THE THIRTEEN COLONIES

North Carolina

CRAIG A. DOHERTY

KATHERINE M. DOHERTY

Facts On File, Inc.

Note on Photos: Many of the illustrations and photographs used in this book are old, historical images. The quality of the prints is not always up to current standards, as in some cases the originals are from old or poor-quality negatives or are damaged. The content of the illustrations, however, made their inclusion important despite problems in reproduction.

Library of Congress Cataloging-in-Publication Data

Doherty, Craig A.
    North Carolina / Craig A. Doherty, Katherine M. Doherty.
        p. cm. — (The Thirteen colonies)
    Includes bibliographical references (p.) and index.
    ISBN 0-8160-5412-6 (acid-free paper)
    1. North Carolina—History—Colonial period, ca. 1600–1775—Juvenile literature. 2.
North Carolina—History—1775–1865—Juvenile literature. I. Doherty, Katherine M. II. Title.

    F257.D64 2005
    975.6'02—dc22   2004010985

Facts On File books are available at special discounts when purchased in bulk quantities for businesses, associations, institutions, or sales promotions. Please call our Special Sales Department in New York at (212) 967-8800 or (800) 322-8755.

You can find Facts On File on the World Wide Web at http://www.factsonfile.com

Text design by Erika K. Arroyo
Cover design by Semadar Megged
Maps and graph by Dale Williams

Printed in the United States of America

VB FOF 10 9 8 7 6 5 4 3 2 1

This book is printed on acid-free paper.

Contents

Introduction

In the 11th century, Vikings from Scandinavia sailed to North America. They explored the Atlantic coast and set up a few small settlements. In Newfoundland and Nova Scotia, Canada, archaeologists have found traces of these settlements. No one knows for sure why the Vikings did not establish permanent colonies. It may have been that it was too far away from their homeland. At about the same time, many Scandinavians were involved with raiding and establishing settlements along the coasts of what are now Great Britain and France. This may have offered greater rewards than traveling all the way to North America.

When the western part of the Roman Empire fell in 476, Europe lapsed into a period of almost 1,000 years of war, plague, and hardship. This period of European history is often referred to as the Dark Ages or Middle Ages. Communication between the different parts of Europe was almost nonexistent. If other Europeans knew about the Vikings' explorations westward, they left no record of it. Between the time of Viking exploration and Christopher Columbus's 1492 journey, Europe underwent many changes.

By the 15th century, Europe had experienced many advances. Trade within the area and with the Far East had created prosperity for the governments and many people. The Catholic Church had become a rich and powerful institution. Although wars would be fought and governments would come and go, the countries of Western Europe had become fairly strong. During this time, Europe rediscovered many of the arts and sciences that had

Vikings explored the Atlantic coast of North America in ships similar to this one. *(National Archives of Canada)*

existed before the fall of Rome. They also learned much from their trade with the Near and Far East. Historians refer to this time as the Renaissance, which means "rebirth."

At this time, some members of the Catholic Church did not like the direction the church was heading. People such as Martin Luther and John Calvin spoke out against the church. They soon gained a number of followers who decided that they would protest and form their own churches. The members of these new churches were called Protestants. The movement to establish these new churches is called the Protestant Reformation. It had a big impact on America because many Protestant groups left Europe so they could worship the way they wanted.

In addition to religious dissent, problems arose with the overland trade routes to the Far East. The Ottoman Turks took control of the lands in the Middle East and disrupted trade. It was at this time that European explorers began trying to find a water route to the Far East. The explorers first sailed around Africa. Then an Italian named Christopher Columbus convinced the king and queen of Spain that it would be shorter to sail west to Asia rather than go around Africa. Most sailors and educated people at the time knew the world was round. However, Columbus made two errors in his calculations. First, he did not realize just how big the Earth is, and second, he did not know that the continents of North and South America blocked a westward route to Asia.

When Columbus made landfall in 1492, he believed that he was in the Indies, as the Far East was called at the time. For a period of time after Columbus, the Spanish controlled the seas and the exploration of what was called the New World. England tried to compete with the Spanish on the high seas, but their ships were no match for the floating fortresses of the Spanish Armada. These heavy ships, known as galleons, ruled the Atlantic.

In 1588, that all changed. A fleet of English ships fought a series of battles in which their smaller but faster and more maneuverable ships defeated the Spanish Armada. This opened up the New World to anyone willing to cross the ocean. Portugal, Holland, France, and England all funded voyages of exploration to the New World. In North America, the French explored the far north. The Spanish had already established colonies in what are now Florida, most of the Caribbean, and much of

Depicted in this painting, Christopher Columbus completed three additional voyages to the Americas after his initial trip in search of a westward route to Asia in 1492. *(Library of Congress, Prints and Photographs Division [LC-USZ62-103980])*

Central and South America. The Dutch bought Manhattan and established what would become New York City, as well as various islands in the Caribbean and lands in South America. The English claimed most of the east coast of North America and set about creating colonies in a variety of ways.

Companies were formed in England and given royal charters to set up colonies. Some of the companies sent out military and trade expeditions to find gold and other riches. They employed men such as John Smith and Bartholomew Gosnold to explore the lands they had been granted. Other companies found groups of Protestants who wanted to leave England and worked out deals that let them establish colonies. No matter what circumstances a

After Columbus's exploration of the Americas, the Spanish controlled the seas, largely because of their galleons, or large, heavy ships, that looked much like this model. *(Library of Congress, Prints and Photographs Division [LC-USZ62-103297])*

colony was established under, the first settlers suffered hardships as they tried to build communities in what to them was a wilderness. They also had to deal with the people who were already there.

Native Americans lived in every corner of the Americas. There were vast and complex civilizations in Central and South America. The city that is now known as Cahokia was located along the Mississippi River in what is today Illinois and may have had as many as 50,000 residents. The people of Cahokia built huge earthen mounds that can still be seen today. There has been a lot of speculation as to the total population of Native Americans in 1492. Some have put the number as high as 40 million people.

Most of the early explorers encountered Native Americans. They often wrote descriptions of them for the people of Europe. They also kidnapped a few of these people, took them back to Europe, and put them on display. Despite the number of Native Americans, the Europeans still claimed the land as their own. European rulers and the Catholic Church at the time felt they had a right to take any lands they wanted from people who did not share their level of technology and who were not Christians.

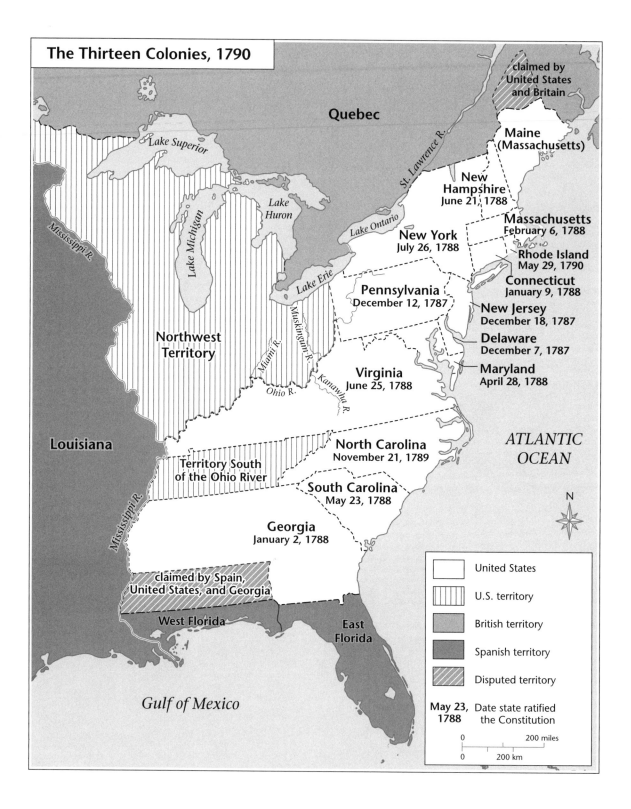

The Thirteen Colonies, 1790

Quebec

claimed by United States and Britain

Lake Superior

Lake Michigan

Lake Huron

Maine (Massachusetts)

St. Lawrence R.

New Hampshire
June 21, 1788

Lake Ontario

Massachusetts
February 6, 1788

New York
July 26, 1788

Lake Erie

Rhode Island
May 29, 1790

Connecticut
January 9, 1788

Pennsylvania
December 12, 1787

New Jersey
December 18, 1787

Northwest Territory

Muskingum R.

Miami R.

Ohio R.

Kanawha R.

Delaware
December 7, 1787

Maryland
April 28, 1788

Mississippi R.

Virginia
June 25, 1788

Louisiana

North Carolina
November 21, 1789

Territory South of the Ohio River

South Carolina
May 23, 1788

ATLANTIC OCEAN

N

Georgia
January 2, 1788

Mississippi R.

claimed by Spain, United States, and Georgia

West Florida

East Florida

Gulf of Mexico

	United States
	U.S. territory
	British territory
	Spanish territory
	Disputed territory

May 23, 1788 Date state ratified the Constitution

0   200 miles

0   200 km

First Contacts

EARLY EXPLORERS

The land that is now North Carolina was an area of conflict-ing claims among the countries of Europe from shortly after Christopher Columbus found his way to the West Indies in 1492 until the mid-1700s. Based on Columbus's voyage, Spain laid claim to most of the Western Hemisphere, and the Spanish were the first to land on the Carolina coast and try to settle there. The English also claimed much of the area. John Cabot sailed west from England in 1497 and explored the coast of North America, from Greenland south. It is believed he headed back to England after sailing south to about 38° latitude, somewhere off the Vir-ginia coast.

Although Cabot probably did not get as far south as the Car-olinas, England claimed the territory anyway. At the time, what a country claimed was not as important as what they could settle and defend. As it turned out, claiming the land of what is today North Carolina was far easier than creating a colony there.

In addition to the Spanish and English, the French also claimed this same area. In 1525, Giovanni de Verrazano, who was an Italian sailing for the French, claimed much of North Amer-ica for France. Over the next 150 years, there were a number of attempts to colonize the area that the Spanish called Carolana, which in Latin means "land of Charles." Charles I was king of

Giovanni da Verrazano sailed to America in 1524 in search of a passageway to China. *(National Archives of Canada)*

Spain at the time, and the land was named in his honor.

In the early 1500s, the Spanish were successful in establishing a number of colonies on the islands of the Caribbean and in Central and South America. Their colonies depended on the enslavement of the Native American people they found there. No one has been able to give an accurate number to the population of Native Americans in 1492. However, the best estimates today suggest that there were far more Native Americans than was previously thought. It is now believed that Hispaniola, which is the second-largest island in the Caribbean, may have had as many as 8 million Native Americans in 1492. However, slavery and European disease reduced that number to a few hundred in less than 100 years.

As the Native American population in the islands was drastically reduced, the Spanish began to import slaves from Africa and Native Americans from other areas. The first documented contact between the Spanish and the Native Americans in Carolana was a voyage in 1521 led by Francisco Gordillo and sponsored by Lucas Vázquez de Ayllón, a government official in Hispaniola. Gordillo sailed with two ships from Hispaniola to the mouth of the Pee Dee River, where the modern town of Georgetown, South Carolina, is situated.

There Gordillo tricked a number of Native Americas onto his ship by offering them gifts. When he had about 150 people on the ship, he sailed off with them. Many of them died on the way to Hispaniola. Gordillo taught Spanish to one of these captives and named him Francisco Chicora. It was Chicora who created interest in settling Carolana by telling stories about his homeland.

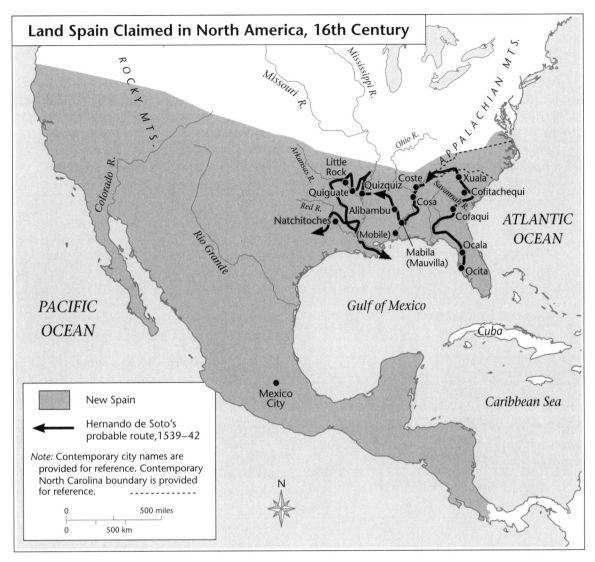

Land Spain Claimed in North America, 16th Century

Legend:
- New Spain
- Hernando de Soto's probable route, 1539–42

Note: Contemporary city names are provided for reference. Contemporary North Carolina boundary is provided for reference. - - - - - - - - - - - -

0 — 500 miles
0 — 500 km

N

Map labels: ROCKY MTS., Missouri R., Mississippi R., Ohio R., APPALACHIAN MTS., Arkansas R., Little Rock, Quizquiz, Coste, Xuala, Cofitachequi, Colorado R., Quiguate, Cosa, Savannah R., Red R., Alibambu, Cofaqui, ATLANTIC OCEAN, Natchitoches, (Mobile), Mabila (Mauvilla), Ocala, Ocita, Rio Grande, PACIFIC OCEAN, Gulf of Mexico, Cuba, Mexico City, Caribbean Sea

Based on the travels of a number of Spanish explorers, Spain claimed a large portion of North America, which included what is now North Carolina.

ATTEMPTED SETTLEMENT

In July 1526, Lucas Vázquez de Ayllón led more than 500 people from the island of Santo Domingo in the Caribbean to Cape Fear. Among the settlers were a number of African slaves who were probably the first Africans in the area that became the thirteen original colonies. They also brought a Native American, Francisco

Francisco Chicora

Francisco Chicora learned to speak Spanish while a prisoner, and he was soon telling amazing stories about the land he came from. The Spanish recorded some of these stories in their journals. One of the most often repeated stories attributed to Chicora was that there was a race of people in Carolana who had long thick tails. To sit down, they had to make a hole in the ground for their tails.

Another story was about a group of giants who got that way by stretching their children. The story the Spanish found most interesting was of the great treasure that existed in Carolana. People today will never know why Chicora told these stories. It may be that he hoped it would somehow get him back to his home, which is what happened. He was taken on the expedition to Carolana to act as a guide and interpreter. As soon as he could, he ran away from the Spanish, who never found the people with tails, giants, or the treasure Chicora had told them about.

Shown in an illustration published in 1892 is Hernando de Soto. With a force of 600 people, he explored what is now the southeastern United States, killing American Indians and destroying villages along the way. *(Library of Congress, Prints and Photographs Division [LC-USZ62-104329])*

Chicora, with them. He had agreed to serve as a guide and interpreter for the group but abandoned them shortly after they arrived at Cape Fear. From the very beginning, this seemed to be an ill-fated attempt at establishing a colony. As the two ships of the expedition entered the Cape Fear River, one of them ran aground and sank. Many of the supplies for the colony were lost.

The colonists soon became sick and realized that the site they had selected was not very healthy. They had set up their camp in the swampy lowlands along the river. Short on supplies and losing members of their group in alarming numbers, the colonists decided to leave Cape Fear and head south. At first they were going to look for a better site. However, as more and more people died, the decision was made to keep going south until they reached the Spanish settlements in Florida. By the time they returned to Santo

Domingo, there were only 150 survivors. It was 1584 before the next attempt was made to establish a colony in what became North Carolina.

Although the Cape Fear colony failed, the Spanish were not ready to give up their claim. They established small communities in what would become South Carolina and explored much of what became the southeastern United States. Hernando de Soto was the leader of the largest expedition of the time. In 1539, he marched north from the west coast of Florida. Before the survivors of this expedition returned, they had traveled more than 4,000 miles and been in what would become the states of South Carolina, North Carolina, Tennessee, Alabama, Mississippi, Arkansas, and Louisiana.

The accounts of de Soto's travels through the area describe the numerous Native Americans who lived there. There were many tribes, and although no accurate estimates of the total number of Native Americans exist, it is believed that more than 35,000 Native Americans lived in the area that is now North Carolina.

Hernando de Soto
(ca. 1496–1542)

De Soto first came to the Americas in 1514 as a soldier assisting Francisco Pizarro in the conquest of the Incas in Peru. For his help in securing the Incan riches for Spain, de Soto was rewarded by being appointed the governor of Cuba. After seeing the wealth of the Incas, de Soto wanted to find his own source of riches and organized an exploration of the southeastern corner of North America.

De Soto failed to find the kind of riches that Hernán Cortés captured in Mexico and that Pizarro stole from the Incas. His small army forced themselves on the Native Americans of the area, stealing food and taking captives wherever they went. They also left behind a trail of European disease, especially smallpox, which eventually killed untold numbers of Native Americans. De Soto also succumbed to disease on the trip. On May 21, 1542, de Soto died near modern-day Natchez, Mississippi. His men were concerned that the Native Americans would attack if they knew de Soto was dead, so they buried him in an unmarked grave and left the area.

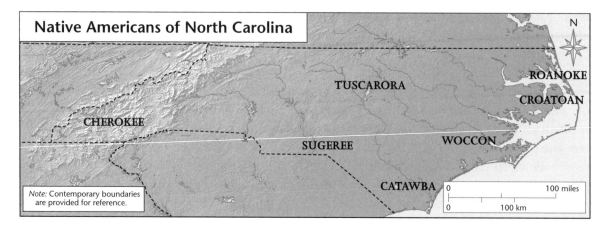

Native Americans of North Carolina

TUSCARORA

ROANOKE

CROATOAN

CHEROKEE

SUGEREE

WOCCON

CATAWBA

Note: Contemporary boundaries are provided for reference.

0   100 miles

0   100 km

N

North Carolina was not an empty wilderness: More than 35,000 Native Americans belonging to a number of different tribes lived in the area.

NATIVE AMERICANS OF NORTH CAROLINA

The Native Americans who lived in present-day North Carolina belonged to numerous tribes that represented three different languages groups. A language group is a number of tribes that speak languages with similar origins. There were approximately 150 language groups in the Americas. Tribes that spoke Algonquian, Siouan, and Iroquoian languages lived in the area.

Two of the most numerous groups in the area spoke Iroquoian languages, which were similar to the languages spoken by the five tribes of the Iroquois Confederacy in what became western New York. These two groups are known as the Cherokee and the Tuscarora. The Tuscarora later moved north and became the sixth member of the League of the Iroquois. The Siouan speakers in the area were the Catawba. In addition to these larger groups, there were some smaller tribes who spoke Algonquian languages and lived along the coastal plain in the northeastern part of the area.

Of the three main groups, the Cherokee were probably the most numerous. They lived in the upland regions of the area. Their territory included the mountains of what are now West Virginia, Virginia, North Carolina, South Carolina, and Georgia. Their territory extended westward into the valleys of what is now eastern Tennessee. The Catawaba lived along the coastal plain in the area that now straddles the border between North and South Carolina.

The Tuscarora originally lived in a large area of the Piedmont of what is now North Carolina and Virginia. They also lived on the coastal plain along the Pamlico, Neuse, and Trent Rivers. After losing a war with British colonists in the early 1700s, the Tuscarora moved north, and it was at that time they joined with the five tribes of the League of the Iroquois.

Native American culture was much more dependent on geography than tribal or language-group association. Therefore, the Native American groups of the area that became North Carolina lived very similar lives. They are considered to be members of the Southeast culture area. They depended on the forests around them for many of the materials needed in their daily lives. Because of their dependence on the forest, another system classifies the tribes of the area into a cultural group known as Eastern Woodlands Indians, merging tribes from the Northeast culture area with some from the Southeast culture area.

THE DAILY LIFE OF NATIVE AMERICANS IN NORTH CAROLINA

Long before Europeans started coming to what would become the Carolinas, the Native Americans of the area were farmers who depended primarily on three crops. The women of the tribe

Corn

Corn was first domesticated 6,000 to 8,000 years ago in Central America. Its cultivation spread until it was grown throughout the temperate regions of North America. Corn is a member of the grass family. Through careful seed selection and hybridization, Native Americans were able to develop many varieties of corn and adapt its growth to a wide range of climatic zones. In North Carolina, the Native Americans grew three main varieties of corn. The most important type could be dried and ground into cornmeal to make a variety of dishes. They also grew a variety of corn that was dried whole and added to soups and stews throughout the winter. It was also eaten fresh, like modern corn on the cob. They also cultivated a type of corn that was used as popcorn.

did most of the farming. They grew corn, beans, and a variety of squashes. These were considered the "Three Sisters" of Native American subsistence.

For most tribes, the Green Corn Festival, when the first corn of the summer became ripe enough to eat, was the most important celebration of the year. It was at this time that the people in a village would give thanks to the spirits of the Three Sisters, who were part of their religion, which included worshipping many different spirits.

In addition to the Three Sisters, the Native Americans of the area grew sunflowers and tobacco. The sunflowers were grown for their seeds. Tobacco was used by most Native Americans as part of their religious observances. During religious ceremonies, they would smoke tobacco in pipes. The purpose of this was to assist their prayers in reaching the spirit world, which they believed was above the sky. Because they were farmers, most of the Native Americans lived in villages along the many rivers and streams of the region. The land along the waterways was richer than the land in the uplands.

All Woodland Indians built their houses in a similar fashion, although there were differences in size and shape among the various groups. The smallest structures were known as wigwams. These structures were made by taking small trees, known as saplings, and burying the thicker ends in a circle in the ground. The tops of the saplings were bent into the center, where they were tied together. The resulting dome was then covered with large sheets of bark to keep out the weather. A hole was left in the center of the roof to let the smoke out of the winter cooking fire. In the warmer weather, most people cooked outdoors.

Some of the larger structures built by Native Americans in this area were built in the same basic manner as a wigwam, but the saplings were placed in an elongated form to make an oval-shaped hut. The Tuscarora, like the Iroquois, built longhouses. To build a longhouse, two rows of saplings were placed in the ground 15 to 20 feet apart. The saplings were then bent to form a long arch. A frame was attached to give the arch strength and to hold the bark covering in place. Some longhouses were more than 100 feet long and housed a number of family groups that were all related.

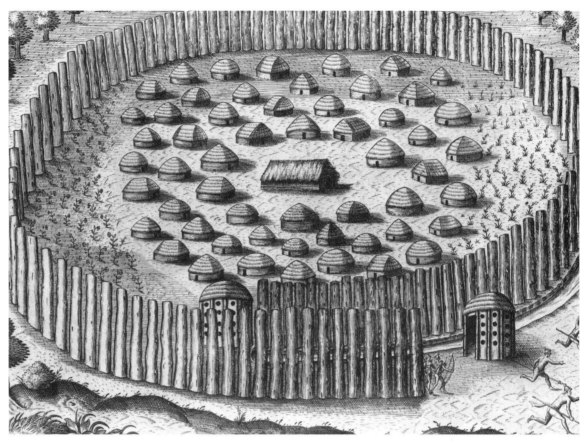

To protect themselves, some tribes built palisades (also called stockades), or a perimeter around their villages made of tall timbers, sharpened at one end and driven into the ground. *(Library of Congress)*

Many of the groups in the area fortified their villages by building a log wall around them called a palisade. The bases of the logs were placed in a trench and buried to make a palisade of upright logs. Often the top end of the logs were sharpened into a point to make it hard for enemies to climb over the wall. There were not many wars between Native American groups. However, small groups of warriors would conduct raids against the villages of opposing groups. Groups would also fight if they were found hunting in an area that was considered the territory of another tribe.

Hunting was an extremely important part of the life of Woodlands Indians. They had no domesticated animals and

Managing Deer Habitat

Today the federal and state governments spend millions of dollars a year trying to maintain and improve habitat for wild animals. Many people think of wildlife management as a fairly modern science. However, when Europeans arrived in the Carolinas, they were surprised to find large tracts of parklike forest that had very little under- growth and was excellent grazing habitat for deer. The Native Americans of the area used fire to minimize the smaller brushy plants and young trees in the forest and improve the habitat for deer. This helped make the deer even more plentiful than they would have been without the intervention of Native Americans in the habitat.

depended on wild game to supplement the food they grew. The most important animal for Woodland Indians was the white-tailed deer. When a deer was killed, all parts of the animal were

American Indians used almost every part of the white-tailed deer that they killed. *(National Park Service)*

utilized. The meat was eaten, the hide was tanned and used for clothes, and the bones and antlers were used to make a number of tools as well as such things as needles. Even the sinew, the fiber surrounding and connecting the muscle tissue, was used for string.

In addition to deer, turkey, bear, and many smaller animals were hunted. When the men were not hunting, they often spent time fishing. Those Native Americans who lived along the bays and rivers of the coastal plain could also gather a variety of shellfish. As the seasons progressed, numerous wild plants were also collected and added to their diet. The women and children would do most of the gathering of berries, nuts, and edible roots when they were ready to be harvested.

Although Native Americans in this area had no written language, they had a rich tradition of storytelling in which they preserved the history and religion of their tribe. Native American religion varied from group to group, but most had similar beliefs. They believed they lived in close proximity to the spirit world, and that all living things and the earth itself were connected by

Cherokee Creation Story

The Cherokee believe that the world was originally covered by water and all living things lived above the sky in a place called Galun'lati. As this place became crowded, the people and animals there began to wonder if they could somehow live in the water world below the sky.

It was decided to send a water beetle down to look for a place they could go. All the water beetle found was ocean. The beetle decided to look under the water and dove down to the bottom. It brought up some mud. When the beetle released the mud, it began to expand until it grew into a flat, soft plain. After the water beetle returned to tell what happened, birds were sent to see if they could move to the land.

The land was very flat, and when they landed, they sank into the mud. Everyone was very discouraged, and they waited a long time before they checked the earth again. This time they sent down the great buzzard to fly over the still soft ground. As it flew low, the power of its wings caused the flat land to form into valleys and ridges. This created the mountain homelands of the Cherokee.

A participant in the French and Indian War, Austenaco was a Cherokee chief during the late 18th century.
(Library of Congress, Prints and Photographs Division [LC-USZ62-90958])

these spirit beings. Through a variety of ceremonies, they gave thanks to the spirits for a successful hunt, for the fish in the rivers that were plentiful and easy to catch, for the ripening of the corn, and many other events in their lives. They also had a complex set of beliefs that described the origins of their people.

The idea that North America was a trackless wilderness waiting for the Europeans to take it was a misconception that came about for a number of reasons. Primary among those was a belief in Europe that people who were not Christians were somehow inferior to those who were. The Native Americans at first welcomed and tried to help the settlers and explorers who came from Europe. They quickly learned that it was going to be difficult to get along with the white settlers and their different sets of beliefs.

The Europeans brought diseases that killed a large percentage of the Native American population. Those Indians who did not die of disease were often forced to leave their traditional home territories. When the Native Americans resisted the encroachment of the Europeans, wars broke out. In North Carolina, in the early 1700s, the Tuscarora War was fought. Eventually, the Native American population of North Carolina was reduced to around 1,000 people.

2

First English Settlements in North Carolina

The establishment of the colony of North Carolina started out badly for the English and then the situation worsened. Queen Elizabeth I ruled England from 1558 until 1603. During her reign, she was forced to confront the growing power and wealth of Spain. Much of Spain's success stemmed from the riches it was bringing to Europe from its colonies in Central and South America. England had claims in the Americas based on some of its early exploration but had not had the strength or resources to do anything about those claims.

Under Elizabeth's guidance, England grew as a maritime power and began to challenge Spanish dominance of the oceans of the world. Numerous English ship captains made fortunes by attacking Spanish shipping. However, it became apparent that to compete with the Spanish and the French,

While Elizabeth I ruled England and Ireland, she supported exploration and colonization efforts and the strengthening of the navy. *(Library of Congress, Prints and Photographs Division [LC-USZ62-120887])*

After Elizabeth I granted Sir Walter Raleigh a charter, Raleigh repeatedly attempted to establish a colony named Virginia in North America. *(Library of Congress, Prints and Photographs Division [LC-USZ6-670])*

who were also pursuing interests in the Americas, England would need its own colonies.

Elizabeth granted a charter to Sir Humphrey Gilbert in June 1578, giving him the right to explore and colonize in North America. On his first trip to North America in 1578, Gilbert accomplished little. He returned in 1583 with a small number of colonists and plans to establish a colony in Newfoundland. After a month in Newfoundland, Gilbert decided to move south to Cape Breton, but he lost one of his ships. He then instructed the rest of the expedition to sail for home. Somewhere in the North Atlantic, they ran into a storm, and the ship Gilbert was on sank and all aboard were lost.

When the ships that survived the storm reached England, the people reported Gilbert's death. The queen then turned to one of her favorites at the court, Sir Walter

The Raleigh Charter
(1584)

The original charter was written in the formal English of the time and is not easily understood by the modern reader. It gave Raleigh the exclusive right to explore and colonize any lands that were not already in the possession of any Christian prince. It allowed Raleigh to govern any colony as he wished as long as he granted the colonists the basic rights that all English people were due.

The charter goes on to grant Raleigh all the land within 200 leagues (350 miles) of any settlements he creates. As payment for the charter, the queen was to receive one-fifth of all the gold and silver the colony produced. The charter allowed Raleigh six years to establish his first permanent colony. Raleigh never found any gold or silver, nor did he succeed in establishing a colony in the allotted time.

When English colonists settled on Roanoke Island, coastal Algonquians now known as the Roanoke lived there. John White, an artist who participated in an effort to colonize the island in 1584, created the image of a Roanoke chief that is the basis for this engraving by Theodor de Bry. *(Library of Congress, Prints and Photographs Division [LC-USZ62-89909])*

Raleigh. Raleigh was Gilbert's half brother, and he was very interested in pursuing his brother's plan of establishing an English colony in North America. In 1584, Elizabeth gave a new charter to Raleigh that gave him the right to explore and colonize in North America.

Raleigh immediately set out to explore the land that he and the queen decided to call Virginia. Because Elizabeth had never been married, she was known as the virgin queen. The new land was named in her honor. Raleigh never actually went to Virginia, but he spent a number of years and large sums of his personal wealth trying to establish a colony there.

The first voyage he outfitted left England on April 27, 1584, with Captains Philip Amadas and Arthur Barlow in charge. On July 4, 1584, they arrived off the coast of North America somewhere in the vicinity of what would become the Carolinas. For the next

John White
(ca. 1540–ca. 1606)

John White's first trip to North America was probably on one of the three voyages to Canada made by Sir Martin Forbisher between 1576 and 1578. People assume this because some of White's earliest known drawings accurately depict the Inuit, who were encountered by the Forbisher expeditions. By 1584, White had become well known as an artist and was hired by Raleigh to record what was seen during the expedition he sponsored.

White continued to make trips to what became North Carolina. In 1587, Raleigh appointed him governor when a third attempt was made to establish a colony in the land Raleigh called Virginia. It was John White's daughter, Eleanor White Dare, who gave birth on August 18, 1587, to the first English child born in North America. The baby was named Virginia.

nine days, they carefully sailed along the coast looking for a bay or river they could safely enter. Somewhere between what are now known as Cape Lookout and Cape Hatteras, they entered Pamlico Sound and went ashore.

Onshore the English captains held a ceremony in which they claimed the land in Queen Elizabeth's name. They set up a base camp on Roanoke Island at the north end of Pamlico Sound. Here they made friendly contact with the local Native Americans. Much of what is known about the way the Native Americans of the area lived and dressed can be attributed to John White, an artist, who was on the first trip to Roanoke Island and would later return as governor of the colony. White's drawings and paintings have been an important source of information and have appeared in hundreds of books.

The first expedition to what would become the Carolinas brought back samples of the plants and animals of the area, as well as numerous objects made by Native Americans. They also brought back two Native Americans, Manteo and Wanchese. All this created quite a stir at Queen Elizabeth's court. With the queen's help, Raleigh made plans to send a group to Virginia to set up a colony.

THE FIRST COLONY

Queen Elizabeth provided the ship the *Tiger* as well as important supplies, especially gunpowder, for the colony. Sir Richard Grenville, Raleigh's cousin, was put in charge, and the queen recalled Ralph Lane from Ireland to serve as the governor of the colony. There was concern that the colony might have to defend itself against the Spanish, who had colonies to the south, so it was organized in a military fashion. As many as 600 men were involved in the expedition. John White was along once again to record in pictures what the colonists found and experienced. The group included 300 soldiers and a number of skilled workers such as carpenters, miners, and metal workers. Apparently, Raleigh expected his colony to discover the same sort of riches the Spanish had found in Central and South America.

The expedition sailed in seven ships from England in April 1585. After a stop in the Caribbean for additional supplies, they arrived at what is now Portsmouth Island during the last week of June 1585. It was here that the colony's bad luck began. While trying to negotiate the passage into Pamlico Sound, the *Tiger* ran aground and was seriously damaged. Many of the supplies on the ship were ruined, and the expedition did not reach its destination on Roanoke Island until the end of July.

The Missing Silver Cup

The history of the relations between Native Americans and English colonists is made up of numerous misunderstandings and atrocities. The pattern was frequently the same. At first, the Native Americans would offer friendship and hospitality. Then, based on a misunderstanding, usually due to cultural differences, the relationship between the two groups would deteriorate. In 1585, problems arose even before the colonists had reached Roanoke Island.

While they waited for the *Tiger* to be repaired, John White and the leaders of the expedition visited many of the Native American villages in the area. At one of the villages, they discovered that one of their silver cups was missing. Without any proof, they assumed that one of the Native Americans had stolen it. In retaliation, the English burned an entire village and its surrounding cornfields.

Built by English colonists in 1585, Fort Raleigh is now a national historic site. The entrance gate to the reconstructed earthen fort is visible in this undated photograph. *(Library of Congress, Prints and Photographs Division [HABS, Nc, 28-Mant.V,1-A-1])*

When they finally reached Roanoke Island, construction was begun on what was to be Fort Raleigh. A number of houses were also built. The leaders of the expedition soon realized that they had a serious problem. Due to the loss of supplies in the *Tiger*, there was not enough food to see the colony through the winter. First, Captain John Arundel was sent to England to make sure more supplies were sent. Grenville had planned to use the *Tiger* to attack Spanish shipping that sailed north along the coast before turning east for Europe, but he was unhappy with the anchorages around Roanoke. He decided to return to England as well.

Lane and 107 men were left at the fort to wait until supplies arrived from England. The supplies did not come, but they somehow managed to make it through the winter. By June, the situation in the colony had become desperate. Supplies had not arrived, but Sir Francis Drake, who had been attacking Spanish colonies in and around the Caribbean, stopped at the colony in June 1586. Lane made a decision to abandon the colony and return to England with Drake.

Three English soldiers who were off exploring were left behind. Drake also left a number of African and Native American slaves he had captured in his raids on Spanish colonies. As Lane and most of his men sailed home on June 19, Grenville was on his way back to Roanoke. When the first of his ships arrived a few days later, it was too late. All they found were two bodies hanging in the fort, one Englishman and one Native American. What happened to the other two Englishmen and the slaves Drake had left behind is not known.

THE SECOND COLONY

When Grenville arrived, he had little interest in staying at Roanoke. He was much more interested in trying to capture one of the Spanish treasure ships that would soon be leaving the Caribbean and heading for Spain. Between 15 and 20 men were left at Roanoke to try and hang on to Fort Raleigh. They were given enough supplies to last them a couple of years, and Grenville sailed off in search of treasure.

At some point during the winter, it is believed that a number of the men were invited to a feast at one of the local Native American villages. This may have been a trap, as some of them were killed by their hosts. A few men who escaped or had not gone are believed to have tried to sail home in a small boat. They were

A few years before he visited the colony at Roanoke Island, Sir Francis Drake circumnavigated the world. *(Library of Congress, Prints and Photographs Division [LC-USZ62-87525])*

never heard from again. This was the second disappearance from Roanoke, but it would not be the last.

THE LOST COLONY

Raleigh was undaunted by the failure of the Lane colony and made plans for another attempt at a colony in North America. This colony included a number of families. John White was appointed governor, and the plan called for them to try a new site farther north in what is now Virginia. However, they were instructed to go to Roanoke and pick up the men Grenville had left behind. When they arrived at Roanoke on July 22, 1587, there were two problems. Fort Raleigh was deserted, and the captain of the ship did not want to sail into the uncharted waters of what would become known as Chesapeake Bay.

Governor White had no choice but to try once more to establish a colony at Roanoke. He and the more than 100 colonists with him set about building more houses and cleaning up the fort. Within a few days of their arrival, one of the colonists, George Howe, was out gathering crabs. Native Americans believed it was acceptable to seek revenge for wrongs done to them. If they could not find the actual person who had acted against them, it was all right to seek revenge against someone from the same family or tribe.

During the time of the Lane colony, one of the chiefs of the Roanoke Indians had been killed by an Englishman. Howe became the object of their revenge, and he was found with 16 arrows sticking out of him. His head had also been bashed in. The attack on an innocent colonist was not to be tolerated by the English. In retribution, Governor White sent out a group to punish the Roanoke. Unfortunately, they came upon a group from the Croatoan tribe and attacked them even though they had not been the ones who killed Howe.

On August 18, 1587, the colonists finally had something to feel good about. The governor's daughter, Eleanor White Dare, gave birth to the first English child to be born in North America. In honor of their new home, the baby was named Virginia. However, what happened to her and the rest of the colonists in Roanoke soon became one of the great mysteries of American history.

In this early 20th-century painting, Virginia Dare, the first English child born in North America, is baptized. *(North Carolina Museum of History)*

As summer 1587 came to an end, it was apparent that the colony was running short of supplies, especially food. The ships that had brought them were about to leave for England. Governor White reluctantly decided to go back to England and make sure that supplies were rushed back to Roanoke. On August 27, 1587, he left his nine-day-old granddaughter and the rest of the colonists behind.

Before he left, White instructed the colonists that, if for any reason they had to leave the area, they were to carve a message on a tree near the fort. If they had to leave because of a threat, they were supposed to carve a cross above the destination. It seems that White was concerned about leaving Roanoke, but he felt he needed to be the one to go back to England.

His plan was to go to England, get supplies, and sail back to Roanoke. However, the situation in England had changed since he had left in the spring. England was preparing for an attack by a huge fleet of Spanish warships known as the Armada. Every available ship in England was commissioned to help defend the country. Despite the impending war, in April 1588, White was allowed to head for Roanoke with two ships that were considered too small to use against the Armada. Unfortunately, they

The Defeat of the Spanish Armada
(July 1588)

Spain and England were enemies for a number of reasons. They were competitors around the world for trade, and many English ship captains had become wealthy by attacking Spanish shipping. An even greater problem was their religious differences. Spain was a staunchly Catholic country. In order to divorce one of his wives, Elizabeth I's father, Henry VIII, forced the English church to break away from the Catholic Church in Rome. Under Elizabeth, England supported Protestants in the Netherlands, which at the time was part of the Spanish Empire.

The king of Spain, Philip, knew it would be hard to solve his problems in the Netherlands without first dealing with the English. He instructed his admirals and generals to come up with a plan to neutralize England. In 1587, a force of 130 ships and 30,000 men were assembled at Cádiz, Spain. The English knew of the plan and were able to delay the attack for a year by harassing any ship that tried to leave Cádiz.

The next year, the Armada was able to set sail for England. On July 29, 1588, a fleet of smaller but more maneuverable English ships met the Armada off the coast near Plymouth, England. For over a week, the English tried to gain the upper hand over the huge warships of the Armada. However, they were unable to break the fighting formation the Spanish used to protect each other. After fighting to a stalemate, the Spanish anchored at Calais, France to take on provisions and make repairs.

The English seized the opportunity and sent a number of ships that they set on fire into the anchorage. The Spanish broke ranks and left Calais in a panic. The English were finally able to defeat the disorganized Spanish fleet in what is known as the Battle of Gravelines. Because of weather conditions, the Spanish ships that were able to escape were forced to sail north. Before they could sail for Spain, they had to sail all the way around Britain and Ireland. Of the 130 ships that had were attacked at sea by French forces and were forced to return to England.

Although the Spanish Armada was defeated in summer 1588, White was not able to get back to Roanoke until summer 1590. When he arrived there, around the time of his granddaughter's third birthday, he found Fort Raleigh abandoned. The only trace of the colonists was carved on two trees. One just had the letters *CRO*. The other tree had the word *CROATOAN* carved on it. There was no

been a part of the Armada, only 67 made it back to Spain.

Although the war continued until 1604, Spain's position as the most powerful military in the world had ended. The English soon claimed that position, and their efforts to colonize in the Americas began in earnest.

The English's 1588 defeat of the Spanish Armada is depicted on the far left of this 17th-century engraving. *(Library of Congress, Prints and Photographs Division [LC-USZ62-86540])*

In this painting, English explorers examine the only trace of the colonists who had inhabited the Roanoke colony John White had governed. *(North Carolina Office of Archives and History)*

cross to symbolize trouble, but there was no other sign of the people White had left behind.

Storms and a lack of supplies made it impossible for White to search for his granddaughter and the rest of the colonists. He was forced to return to England without solving the mystery. There is no actual proof, but many historians have come to the conclusion that the lost colony moved north and settled with a group of Native Americans in the area of what is now Norfolk, Virginia. It is also believed that Powhatan, a Native American leader who controlled much of the area that became Virginia, probably attacked the village that was helping the colonists and killed them all.

Roanoke and the Story Tree Rings Tell

Although no one has proved what happened to the "lost colony" at Roanoke, modern scientists have discovered one fact that may have contributed to the colony's disappearance and the difficulties that the next group of settlers had at Jamestown, Virginia. Through the process of dendrochronology, scientists can date the age of trees by studying tree-growth rings. They also discover patterns of weather over long periods of time by the width of each ring. Using Bald Cypress trees, some of which are more than 1,000 years old, scientists have been able to determine the amount of rainfall far back into the prehistorical period of North America.

They have discovered that the most severe drought in more than 800 years was at its worst during the time the English were trying to settle Roanoke. A second period of drought coincided with the first years of the colony at Jamestown. Although there is no proof that the drought caused the disappearance of the lost colony, it is likely it was a contributing factor.

Prosperous colonies would be created in Virginia and in what would become South Carolina, but North Carolina was neglected for quite a while. When Queen Elizabeth died in 1603, Sir Walter Raleigh lost his main supporter. The new king, James I, charged Raleigh with treason. Raleigh was convicted and spent the last 13 years of his life locked up in the Tower of London. James I gave the Carolinas to a new group responsible for developing the area.

3

Lost in the Middle

After the loss of the Roanoke colony; it was more than 50 years before there were any permanent European settlers in what is now North Carolina. There were a number of reasons for this. Among them were a new king in England and changes to the charter. But more than anything, the geography of the area made other areas more attractive for colonization.

The most successful colonies in the 17th century were those with a good harbor. Boston, Massachusetts; New York, New York; Philadelphia, Pennsylvania; Baltimore, Maryland; and Charleston, South Carolina, are all important harbors even today. In the 1600s, they all became the economic hub of their colonies. Virginia, which would become the most populous and prosperous colony, had an added advantage. Many of its rivers were wide and deep enough to allow oceangoing ships to sail right up to the large plantations that developed there and load the tobacco and other crops they grew.

In the area that became North Carolina, there were no good harbors. A look at the North Carolina coast shows a series of narrow islands separated from the mainland by numerous shallow bays and sounds. This made it very difficult for oceangoing ships to land in North Carolina. It is also an area often battered by storms. It was a place much better suited for hiding pirates than it was for the trade that was needed for a successful colony.

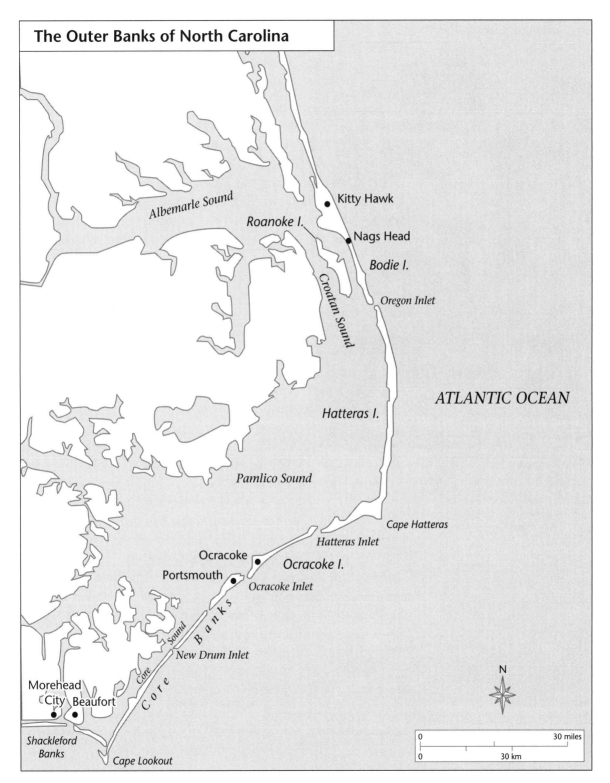

The Outer Banks of North Carolina

Albemarle Sound

Kitty Hawk

Roanoke I.

Nags Head

Bodie I.

Croatan Sound

Oregon Inlet

ATLANTIC OCEAN

Hatteras I.

Pamlico Sound

Cape Hatteras

Hatteras Inlet

Ocracoke

Ocracoke I.

Portsmouth

Ocracoke Inlet

Core Sound

Banks

New Drum Inlet

Core Banks

Morehead City

Beaufort

Shackleford Banks

Cape Lookout

N

| 0 | | 30 miles |
| 0 | 30 km | |

The shifting sands of the Outer Banks made the coast of North Carolina a treacherous place for shipping.

King of Scotland from infancy, King James I inherited the English throne when Elizabeth I died in 1603 and ruled England and Ireland until his death in 1625.
(Library of Congress, Prints and Photographs Division [LC-USZ62-105812])

Despite the fact that the right to colonize the area would switch hands a number of times, no direct attempts at developing the area took place during the 1600s.

CHANGING CHARTERS

Raleigh's original charter of 1584 gave him six years to establish a permanent colony. Since he failed to do that and because a new ruler came to the throne, his rights to land in North America ended. Under the new king, James I, another charter was issued on April 10, 1606, for the area known as Virginia. This charter was granted to two separate companies made up of wealthy men. The first company consisted of investors from London and had the southern half of the lands described in the charter. The other group was made up of merchants from Bristol, Exeter, and Plymouth who would control the northern part of the land.

This charter included all the land for 100 miles inland from the coast between 34° and 41° north latitude, from present-day Cape Fear, North Carolina, north to Bangor, Maine. The London Virginia Company concentrated its efforts on the colony it began in Jamestown, Virginia, in 1607. The Plymouth Virginia Company's efforts centered on what would become Massachusetts. Although the area that is now North Carolina was part of the Virginia Charter, the Company did not do anything about that section of their lands.

The Virginia Company failed to realize the profits that investors had expected and broke into a number of quarrelling factions. In 1624, King James stepped in and revoked their charter. The case went to court and the king won. The lands in North America that had been granted to the Virginia Company came

The Opening Paragraphs of the First Charter of Virginia
(April 10, 1606)

JAMES, by the Grace of God, King of England, Scotland, France and Ireland, Defender of the Faith, &c. WHEREAS our loving and well-disposed Subjects, Sir Thorn as Gales, and Sir George Somers, Knights, Richard Hackluit, Clerk, Prebendary of Westminster, and Edward-Maria Wingfield, Thomas Hanharm and Ralegh Gilbert, Esqrs. William Parker, and George Popham, Gentlemen, and divers others of our loving Subjects, have been humble Suitors unto us, that We would vouchsafe unto them our Licence, to make Habitation, Plantation, and to deduce a colony of sundry of our People into that part of America commonly called VIRGINIA, and other parts and Territories in America, either appertaining unto us, or which are not now actually possessed by any Christian Prince or People, situate, lying, and being all along the Sea Coasts, between four and thirty Degrees of Northerly Latitude from the Equinoctial Line, and five and forty Degrees of the same Latitude, and in the main Land between the same four and thirty and five and forty Degrees, and the Islands hereunto adjacent, or within one hundred Miles of the Coast thereof;

And to that End, and for the more speedy Accomplishment of their said intended Plantation and Habitation there, are desirous to divide themselves into two several Colonies and Companies; the one consisting of certain Knights, Gentlemen, Merchants, and other Adventurers, of our City of London and elsewhere, which are, and from time to time shall be, joined unto them, which do desire to begin their Plantation and Habitation in some fit and convenient Place, between four and thirty and one and forty Degrees of the said Latitude, alongst the Coasts of Virginia, and the Coasts of America aforesaid: And the other consisting of sundry Knights, Gentlemen, Merchants, and other Adventurers, of our Cities of Bristol and Exeter, and of our Town of Plimouth, and of other Places, which do join themselves unto that Colony, which do desire to begin their Plantation and Habitation in some fit and convenient Place, between eight and thirty Degrees and five and forty Degrees of the said Latitude, all alongst the said Coasts of Virginia and America, as that Coast lyeth:

back under the control of the Crown. King James I died in 1625, and it fell to his successor, Charles I, to deal with the new status of the North American colonies.

Charles I quickly asserted his control over the land in North America claimed by England. On October 30, 1629, Charles I rewarded his attorney general, Robert Heath, with a huge section of North America. All the land between 31° and 36° north latitude from the Atlantic Coast to the Pacific Ocean became the personal domain of Heath. This included all the

Charles I ruled England, Scotland, and Ireland from 1625 until his execution in 1649. *(Library of Congress, Prints and Photographs Division [LC-USZ62-91613])*

land from about 50 miles south of the current Florida-Georgia border north to Albemarle Sound just below the current border between Virginia and North Carolina. This land was named Carolana (Latin for "the land of Charles"), after the king.

Heath at first attempted to establish a colony with French Huguenots who had been expelled from France. These were Protestants who found themselves in conflict with the Catholic authority of France. When Parliament passed a law requiring that colonists belong to the Church of England, Heath found 40 English settlers to send to Carolana. When the colonists arrived in Jamestown before moving south to their new home, they changed

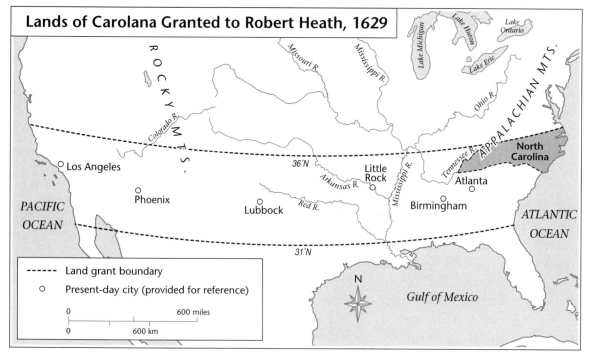

The original English charter included all the land between 31° and 36° north latitude and went from the Atlantic Ocean to the Pacific Ocean.

Nathaniel Batts
(ca. 1620–1679)

In 1655, Nathaniel Batts became the first permanent settler in what is now North Carolina. He established a pattern that was later followed by the majority of early settlers in North Carolina. Batts had been employed on a large plantation owned by Francis Yeardley near Lynnhaven, Virginia. The records are not clear, but it is believed that Batts moved south still in the employ of Yeardley, who sent one of his carpenters to build Batts a house that was 20 feet square and consisted of two rooms. The house was located at the western end of Albemarle Sound, where Salmon Creek enters the sound.

Batts's purpose in moving to what was considered the frontier of Virginia was to establish a trading post and trade with the Native Americans of the area. From land deeds recorded in Virginia, it is known that Batts bought land in the area from Kiscutanewh, the leader of the Yoepim tribe. Visitors to the area in 1672 wrote of meeting Batts and referred to him as the governor of Roanoke.

their minds. Some returned to England while others stayed in Virginia.

Heath gave up his claim to Carolana and transferred it to Henry Frederick Howard, Lord Maltravers, in 1638. Charles I was starting to have difficulties ruling England, and that contributed to a lack of energy for developing the American colonies. In 1649, Charles I was overthrown in a civil war that pitted Puritan forces against those loyal to the king. When the Puritan Oliver Cromwell became the Lord Protector of England, he and his followers executed the king.

During the time of Puritan control in England, many colonies continued to grow, but little happened in the area that would become North Carolina. It was not until 1655 that Nathaniel Batts became the first permanent resident in North Carolina. By 1650, there were already more than 14,000 colonists in Massachusetts and more than 18,000 in Virginia. It was another 70 years before there were that many people in North Carolina.

After Batts arrived, he was followed by others from Virginia. Many of these early settlers in the Albemarle Sound area left Virginia because they could not afford to buy land there. Others left for the frontier to escape debt. Still others were fugitives who

Many of the first English colonists to leave Virginia and settle in North Carolina built small log cabins similar to this one near present-day Harrells, North Carolina. *(Library of Congress, Prints and Photographs Division [HABS, NC,82-KER.V,1-1])*

had committed crimes in Virginia. Within five years, there may have been as many as 1,000 settlers living in the area.

THE RETURN OF THE KING

In 1660, another upheaval took place in the government in England. Oliver Cromwell had died, and his followers were soon faced with forces who had remained loyal to Charles I's exiled son. In 1660, the monarchy was restored in England, and Charles II returned to England as the new king. Charles II had many loyal followers he needed to reward for helping him regain the throne lost by his father.

He lavishly handed out new titles and lands throughout the British Empire. For eight loyal noblemen, the reward was the lands of Carolana that had originally been granted to Robert Heath by Charles I. It was at this time that the spelling of the name was changed to Carolina. The eight men were called the Lords Proprietors. They were Sir John Colleton; Sir William Berkeley; Anthony Ashley Cooper, Lord Ashley; Edward Hyde, earl of Clarendon; George Monck, duke of Albemarle; John, Lord Berkeley, brother of William; Sir George Carteret; and William, earl of Craven.

The Lords Proprietors announced they were dividing Carolina into three counties. The southernmost county was called Craven. It contained most of the early settlement in what would become South Carolina. The middle county was called Clarendon and was mostly in what became the southeastern part of North Carolina.

Charles II granted the lands of Carolina to eight English noblemen in a 1663 charter. Shown here, the original document was purchased by the state of North Carolina in 1949 from an antiquarian bookseller. *(North Carolina Museum of History)*

The northern county was called Albemarle, and it would become the center of settlement in North Carolina.

The Lords Proprietors were permitted by their charter to rule Carolina as they saw fit. They were also expecting to collect money called quitrents from anyone who settled in Carolina. Settlers soon began arriving in Craven and Clarendon Counties. The settlements in Clarendon were quickly abandoned, and that part of Carolina remained empty of European settlers for a long time. In Albemarle County, people continued to arrive from Virginia.

As was the custom in the colonies at the time, a governor was appointed in Albemarle County by the proprietors. They also appointed a council to aid the governor in running the colony. In addition, provisions were made for an elected assembly to represent the people. In Albemarle County, there was almost immediate conflict between the proprietors, represented by the governor and council, and the colonists. Most of the people living in the area had arrived before the proprietors attempted to assert their claim to Carolina. These early settlers resented the proprietary government meddling in their affairs and trying to collect quitrents. The king may have returned to London, but it was difficult to enforce his charters on the frontiers of the American colonies.

Tobacco, the plant in this 18th-century drawing, was an important crop to many in the Carolina colony. *(National Archives of Canada)*

LIFE IN ALBEMARLE COUNTY

By 1670, there were more than 5,000 people in Albemarle County, Carolina. That number would almost double in the next 30 years. However, more people did not mean prosperity. Albemarle did not have its own port, and new regulations passed

Navigation Acts
(1651–1696)

Starting in 1651, Parliament passed a series of laws that were intended to regulate trade between England and its colonies around the world. The First Navigation Acts in 1651 stated that all goods imported into England had to be brought in on English ships. The Staples Act, passed in 1663, further required that any European goods headed to the colonies in America had to be shipped from English ports. The Plantation Duty Act of 1673 created a number of taxes on goods imported into the colonies. It also created posts for customs officers who were responsible for collecting the customs duties. Had the merchants throughout the colonies adhered to the Navigation Acts, they would have soon been out of business, as the added costs of using only English ships and the high duties would have made the costs of imported goods too high. It would have also cut deeply into the colonists' profits on the produce of their farms, forests, and plantations. Smuggling became an accepted practice throughout the colonies. Although no one really thought of it in these terms at the time, defying the Navigation Acts was the first small step toward declaring independence more than 100 years later.

by Parliament made it difficult for the farmers of the area to sell their produce at a profit. The farmers in Albemarle worked hard growing corn, tobacco, and a number of other crops, but it was difficult to get goods to market.

It was a long way overland to the ports of Virginia, and once people got their goods there, they had to pay large fees to ship their goods because they were not grown in Virginia. Some of the tobacco that was grown in Albemarle was sent out in smaller ships to Scotland, Ireland, France, Holland, and Spain. However, the attempts to enforce the Plantation Duty Act of 1673 and other aspects of the Navigation Acts made that trade illegal. Many in Albemarle were forced to turn to smuggling to find markets for their tobacco.

It took until the 1800s for the tobacco growers of North Carolina to compete with their wealthier neighbors in Virginia. Albemarle remained a place of relatively poor farmers with very few slaves. In Virginia to the north and Craven County to

Published in *Frank Leslie's Illustrated Newspaper,* this illustration details the complicated process involved in cultivating and harvesting rice. In this illustration, black slaves plant, hoe, weed, reap, and thresh rice. *(Library of Congress, Prints and Photographs Division [LC-USZ62-96954])*

the south, large numbers of slaves were imported to provide cheap labor for the plantation culture that developed in the late 1600s.

CULPEPER'S REBELLION

The people of Albemarle quickly divided into two groups. One group supported the governor and council. These people were loyal to the Lords Proprietors. On the other side was the majority of the people in the area who had arrived before the proprietary government was formed. They felt they were represented best by the elected assembly. The supporters of the governor and council tried to make the rest of the population follow the laws of Parliament and the Lords Proprietors.

In spite of the Navigation Acts, trade had developed between the tobacco growers of North Carolina and merchants from New England. These merchants tended to use smaller ships than their British counterparts. This allowed them to more easily navigate the treacherous waters of Albemarle Sound. The customs collectors at the time looked the other way and did not interfere with this trade. However, the situation changed radically when Thomas Miller was appointed deputy governor in 1677.

Miller was loyal to the proprietors and had been ill-treated by the people of Albemarle in the past. He had been put in jail by Governor Jenkins, who was a supporter of the anti-proprietor faction in the colony. After escaping from jail and going to England to report on conditions in the colony, Miller returned to Albemarle. His actions would indicate that it was his intention to get even with the people who had jailed him.

He quickly took advantage of his posting as deputy governor to assert the full authority of the governor's office, as the actual governor had not arrived yet. He had his enemies jailed and appointed himself customs and tax collector. Many people were upset with Miller. When he seized the New England trading ship the *Carolina*, the people of Albemarle had had enough. With John Culpeper as their leader, Albemarle's citizens put Miller in jail and took over the colony.

Culpeper acted as governor for the next two years, and the people of Albemarle happily went about their business without any interference from the proprietors or anyone else in England. This brief period of political tranquility might have continued had Miller not escaped from jail and fled to England. To be sure the proprietors and other officials in London got both sides of the story, Culpeper followed Miller to England.

When Culpeper arrived in England, he was immediately arrested and charged with treason. Rather than have it seem that the situation was totally out of control in Albemarle, the proprietors defended Culpeper. In fact, one of them, Lord Ashley (later the first earl of Shaftesbury), went so far as to defend him at his trial. Culpeper was acquitted and allowed to return to Albemarle.

The whole incident is referred to as Culpeper's Rebellion and is the first direct action against English authority in the colonies. It pointed out that colonial government was only as good as the governor appointed to head it. Miller had been a bad choice. The next governor, after Culpeper's Rebellion, proved to be even worse.

SETH SOTHEL

After Culpeper was acquitted, the proprietors appointed Seth Sothel the next governor of Albemarle County, Carolina. Sothel had recently bought out Edward Hyde's share of the proprietorship and was intent on profiting from his position as a proprietor. However, on his way from England to his new post, Sothel was captured by pirates. He stayed among the pirates for five years until he finally escaped and made it to Albemarle in 1683.

For the next six years, Sothel used his position as governor to take care of himself and those who supported him. He ignored the existing laws, took bribes when it suited him, and threw anyone who disagreed with him in jail. In 1689, after six years of corruption, the assembly arrested Governor Sothel and put him on trial. When the other proprietors in England heard the details of how their partner had been operating in Albemarle, they had to side with the assembly. They even sent a formal apology to the people of Albemarle. Sothel was expelled from Albemarle but headed south to Charleston in Craven County, where he used his power as a proprietor to become governor there.

NORTH CAROLINA IS CREATED

After a similar fate met Sothel in Charleston, the proprietors appointed a new governor for Carolina based in Charleston and

North Carolina's First Town

In the 115 years since Sir Walter Raleigh had first sent people to Roanoke Island, no real towns had developed in Albemarle County. The people lived independently on their own farms and had not congregated in any towns. That finally changed around 1705, when a group of French Huguenots arrived in the Pamlico River area. A town was laid out by the English surveyor John Lawson. He called it Bath, after the city in England that was home to one of the proprietors. Bath never grew much, and today only has about 200 residents.

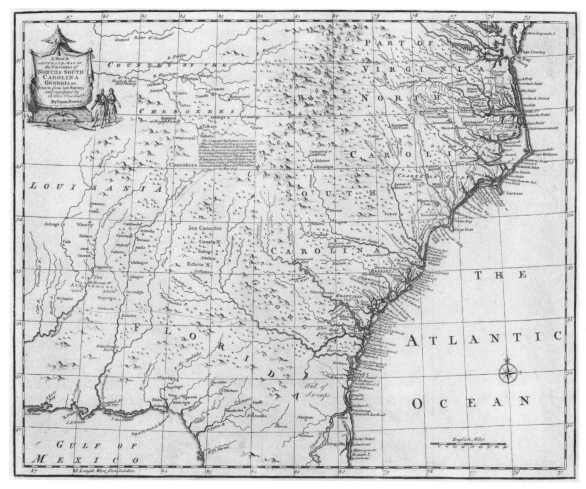

This map of the colonies of North Carolina, South Carolina, and Georgia was published in London in a 1752 atlas. It includes such details as the coastline and the area's rivers. *(Library of Congress, Geography and Map Division)*

attempted to rule Albemarle with a lieutenant governor who answered to the governor. This did not work well either. Albemarle was growing and had spread inland and south to Pamlico Sound. By 1710, there were more than 15,000 people in the northern part of Carolina.

It was time to separate the two Carolinas. Starting in 1712, North Carolina was given its own governor, and the terms North and South Carolina started to be used. But before North Carolina could grow, they would have to resolve their differences with the Tuscarora.

4

Indian Wars and Pirates

From the first misunderstanding over a missing silver cup in 1585, relations between the colonists in the Carolinas and the Native Americans resulted in many conflicts. A number of people in the Carolinas, especially in the southern part of the colony, were involved in capturing Native Americans and selling them as slaves to the plantations in the Caribbean. Others used Native American slaves on their Carolina plantations. In addition, the Europeans brought a number of diseases with them that had a devastating effect on Native Americans. The Europeans also felt they could take any land they wanted.

In some instances, land was acquired from Native Americans by treaty or was purchased by individuals. Even when Europeans had good intentions, these land transactions often caused problems. First, the two cultures had different ideas about land usage. Native Americans had loosely described areas that would be considered the home territory of a given tribe. However, there was no private ownership of land among Native Americans. Also, treaties and land deeds were always written in English, as none of the Native Americans had written languages at this time. Because of this, they often signed documents with no real understanding of what they were giving away.

As more and more people moved into Carolina, the Native Americans were forced to give up the lands along the coast. As time went by, colonists began to move inland, taking more and

Native Americans and Disease

Most scholars agree that the ancestors of the Native Americans originated in Asia and traveled to North America when the two continents were connected by a land bridge between modern-day Siberia and Alaska. During the thousands of years they were isolated from the Asian and European continents, they lost or never developed any immunity to the diseases the Europeans brought with them to North America.

Common diseases for Europeans such as mumps and measles were often fatal to Native Americans. The most deadly disease, which had also killed large numbers of people in Europe, was smallpox. Smallpox epidemics ran through the Native American population of Carolina numerous times during the colonial period. Very few Native Americans survived smallpox. In addition to European diseases, two other

(continues)

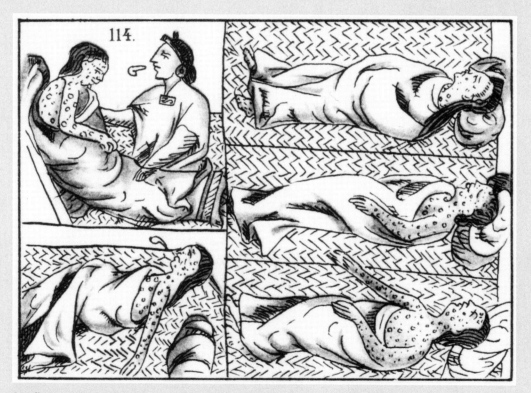

Smallpox and measles, among other diseases that European explorers brought to North America, killed numerous American Indians. In this detail of a drawing from *Historia general de las cosas de Nueva España,* Aztec people in Mesoamerica are infected with smallpox. *(Library of Congress)*

(continued)

deadly diseases, yellow fever and malaria, plagued both the non-Indians and American Indians of Carolina.

Yellow fever and malaria are diseases that are spread by mosquitoes. They originated in Africa and arrived in the Americas via the slave trade. The swamps of coastal Carolina became breeding grounds for disease-carrying insects that infected people of all races. Many Europeans, Africans, and even more Native Americans died from these diseases.

more Native American territory. When Europeans first arrived in North America, they were greeted with the hospitality that was the custom among Native Americans. Had the Native Americans risen up as a group and repelled the first attempts to establish colonies, the history of the United States might have been very different. As it was, by the time the Native Americans realized they were in trouble, it was too late. There were simply far too many colonists and conflicts. The slave trade and disease had greatly reduced the number of Native Americans able to resist European expansion into the interior of Carolina and other colonies.

THE TUSCARORA WAR

Throughout the early years of the 18th century, the relations between European colonists and Native Americans in Carolina continued to worsen. The arrival of new settlers and the establishment of communities like New Bern eventually forced the Tuscarora and a number of smaller tribes allied with them to attack the white settlements.

On September 22, 1711, 500 Tuscarora and their allies attacked outlying farms all along the frontier of North Carolina. In those first dawn raids, more than 140 colonists were killed and another 25 were taken prisoner. At first they did not attack New Bern. Just before the war started, Baron Christoph von Graffenried (see sidebar on page 43) had been captured by the Tuscarora as he and the surveyor John Lawson were exploring to the west of New Bern. Lawson was tortured and executed. Graffenried was able to barter for his life and offered the neutrality of himself and the people of New Bern in exchange for his life and his freedom.

By the time Graffenried got back to New Bern, the people there were too upset by the attacks on their neighbors to go along with the deal Graffenried had made. They tried to retaliate against the Tuscarora, but instead they just turned the warriors against them. No one was safe from the continuing raids by the Tuscarora and their allies. All of North Carolina was in a state of siege, and people were so concerned about protecting their homes and families that they stayed home instead of organizing attacks against the Tuscarora.

The leaders in North Carolina appealed to Governor Spotswood of Virginia for help. Spotswood agreed to send soldiers as long as North Carolina agreed to provide food and other supplies for the troops. However, the Tuscarora had burned most of the crops in North Carolina and either killed or run off most of the livestock. There was no extra food for the Virginia soldiers, so they stayed home. The people of North Carolina then turned to their neighbors in South Carolina.

The leaders in Charleston were willing to help. They voted money for an expedition against the Tuscarora. Colonel John Barnwell was put in charge. He raised a force of 35 colonists and around 500 Yamasee Indians. They marched more than 300 miles to fight against the Tuscarora.

New Bern

Although only a few settlers came directly from England to settle in North Carolina, colonists from other European countries move to the area. Bath had been settled by French Huguenots. Then in 1710, a Swiss land company sent a large group of Swiss and German colonists to start a community in Carolina. About 40 miles south of Bath, where the Neuces and Trent Rivers meet, the leader of the Swiss,

Baron Christoph von Graffenried, negotiated for more than 17,000 acres of land for a community they called New Bern. Although Graffenried had promised the proprietors that he would bring 650 people to New Bern, the community was started with approximately 400 colonists. Their arrival in an area claimed by the Tuscarora is seen as the spark for the Tuscarora War.

The Yamasee War

During the Tuscarora War, the Yamasee fought with the colonists from South Carolina against the Tuscarora. The two Native American groups had long been rivals, and the Yamasee saw this as a way to gain help from the whites against the Tuscarora. If the Yamasee had not helped the colonists, the Tuscarora might have been able to put an end to North Carolina. Looking back, the Yamasee probably regretted fighting against the Tuscarora. In 1715, the Yamasee turned against their South Carolina allies and almost succeeded in driving all the whites out of South Carolina. Had the Yamasee and Tuscarora acted together, both the colonies in North and South Carolina might have been driven back out of the area.

Barnwell's campaign killed many Tuscarora and burned a number of towns. In spring 1712, Barnwell made peace with the Tuscarora and convinced them to move westward away from the European settlements. The peace treaty might have held, except for the Yamasee. They were not interested in peace with the Tuscarora and captured a group of Native Americans who were allies of the Tuscarora, taking them off to be sold as slaves. The peace treaty was broken, and the Tuscarora resumed their attacks on the whites of North Carolina.

This time when North Carolina asked for help, South Carolina sent a force of colonists and 1,000 Native Americans. A force of 200 North Carolinians joined them. Colonel James Moore of South Carolina was put in charge. In March 1713, a bloody battle was fought near present-day Snow Hill, North Carolina. During the battle, more than 1,000 Tuscarora were either killed or captured. On the other side, the colonists lost only 60 fighters. This put an end to the Tuscarora War, and the Tuscarora left North Carolina to join their relatives, the Iroquois, in what is now western New York.

The end of the Tuscarora War resulted in the inland areas of the colony becoming safe for expansion. However, the waters off Carolina were some of the most dangerous in the world. There were many dangerous shoals and many violent storms, but the main danger to ships sailing along the coast were pirates.

PIRATE HAVEN

The long coast of the Carolinas with its dangerous sandbars and many bays and islands was the perfect hiding place for pirates who attacked the numerous ships that sailed up and down the Atlantic coast of North America. Not only was the Carolina coast the ideal place for pirates to hide, it appears that officials and residents in both the north and south ends of the Carolinas were sympathetic to the pirates.

Born Edward Teach, Blackbeard earned his nickname as a result of his thick, black beard. This image of the pirate originally appeared in an early 18th-century book titled *A General History of Pyrates*. *(North Carolina Museum of History)*

The goods the pirates stole from ships found a ready market in the Carolinas, where the struggling colonists were happy to pay bargain prices for stolen goods that would not have been available through legitimate trade. Even if the goods had been coming into the colony by legal means, most of the people, especially the people in the north, would not have been able to afford them at full price. In addition to providing a market for the pirates' stolen booty, the people of the colony sold the pirates food and other supplies.

There was little real money in the colonies. The pirates usually paid in silver and gold coins. This much-needed cash was apparently more important to the colony than how it was obtained. It is reported that a number of officials in North Carolina profited from the trade with pirates by taking bribes to ignore the pirates' illegal activities.

Blackbeard
(Edward Teach, ca. 1680–1718)

Edward Teach, who was known by the nickname Blackbeard, may have been one of the most savage pirates in America. He reportedly would cut off a captive's finger if he or she refused to give up a ring that he wanted. He started his career as a privateer in the employ of the English. When Queen Anne's War ended in 1713, he continued to attack shipping as a pirate.

He is reported to have said, "Come let us make a Hell of [our] own, and try how long we can bear it."

Blackbeard got his name from his wild black beard. He would braid it for battle and position a fuse known as a slow-match so it would hang out from under his hat. He would light the fuse during battles, so he would be followed by a cloud of smoke that must have made him look like the devil many believed him to be. Despite his devilish appearance in battle, he must have seemed attractive to some of the women of the Carolinas and the Caribbean. It is reported that he married 14 times without ever getting a divorce, although many of the marriages were performed by one of his crewmen, who had no authority to perform the ceremony.

For a time, Blackbeard used Ocracoke Island, one of the barrier islands that make up the North Carolina coast, as his headquarters. At times, large groups of pirates would gather there for parties that would go on for days. Blackbeard may have been at his most formidable during his alliance with the pirate Stede Bonnet.

Many well-known pirates operated in the waters of Carolina. One of the most famous was Blackbeard. Stede Bonnet, Captain Kidd, "Calico Jack" Rackham, and many others also frequented the Carolina coast. Many of the pirates had started out as privateers during Queen Anne's War. *Privateer* was the term used to describe private ships and sailors employed by governments to attack the shipping of their enemies. After the war, as the plantations of South Carolina became more prosperous, the pirate Blackbeard and others started attacking ships sailing into and out of Charleston.

Between the years 1689 and 1762, France and England fought against each other in four wars. During each of these wars, both sides employed privateers to attack the shipping of the other side. In the times between the wars, some of these privateers would turn from legally attacking enemy shipping to operating as pirates and attacking merchant ships no matter who owned them. After Queen Anne's War

One of Captain Robert Maynard's sailors killed Blackbeard after a fierce battle, depicted in this image from an early 19th-century book about pirates. *(Library of Congress, Prints and Photographs Division [LC-USZ62-86666])*

(1702–13), the authorities in Virginia and South Carolina wanted to put an end to piracy along their coasts.

In South Carolina, people were especially upset with Blackbeard. In 1718, Blackbeard brought his force right into the entrance to Charleston Harbor, where he waylaid ships and took hostages. When he finally left Charleston, the governor sent Colonel William Rhett to put an end to piracy in the Carolinas. After a sea battle, Rhett captured Stede Bonnet and a number of his pirate crew near the mouth of the Cape Fear River. Bonnet and his men were brought back to Charleston, where he and 50 of his men were hanged.

Blackbeard was a little harder to capture. After attacking the shipping at Charleston, he rushed back to his base in North Car-

Women Pirates

Anne Bonny was born in Cork, Ireland. Her father, William Cormac, was a prominent attorney, and her mother was Peg Brennan, one of the maids in Cormac's household. When Cormac's wife discovered his affair with the maid, and that she was carrying his child, Cormac and Brennan left Ireland and moved to Charleston, Carolina, where he became a wealthy lawyer, merchant, and planter. Soon after they arrived in Charleston, their daughter Anne was born.

Anne grew up preferring riding and hunting to traditional activities expected of a young girl. In her late teens, her father arranged a marriage for her to a member of a well-respected family in Charleston. Instead of accepting her arranged marriage, Anne eloped with a young sailor named James Bonny. She soon left Bonny for the pirate Calico Jack Rackham. Rather than stay ashore as most pirate girlfriends and wives did, Anne disguised herself as a man and joined the crew.

Rackham and his crew captured a merchant ship and the crew was forced to join the pirates. When Anne seemed to be paying undue attention to one of the new crew members, Calico Jack became jealous. Anne was forced to reveal that she was a woman, and so was the captured crew member, Mary Read. After that, the two women stayed members of the pirate crew without having to disguise themselves as men.

When Rackham's ship was captured in Jamaica, he and most of his crew were executed. Anne and Mary were examined by a doctor, who declared that they were both pregnant. Their sentences were commuted and Anne is known to have returned to Carolina. Some believe that her father may have bribed the doctor to help the two women avoid the gallows.

olina, where he was granted a pardon by the governor, Charles Eden. Most likely Eden received a large bribe to pardon his pirate friend. Virginia's Governor Spotswood was fed up with the pirates who were interfering with trade there. He did not care about the North Carolina pardon and sent out a force commanded by British naval lieutenant Robert Maynard.

Maynard sailed to Ocracoke Island and found Blackbeard. After a running battle between the two forces that saw many casualties on both sides, Blackbeard was killed by one of Maynard's sailors just as he was about to finish off the navy man. Maynard had Blackbeard's head removed and carried it back to Virginia as proof that the pirate would never attack another merchant ship.

With the deaths of Blackbeard and Bonnet, the number of pirates operating in Carolina was drastically reduced. Those who were not killed in battles were executed. Those pirates who escaped fled to other areas of operation in the Caribbean and the island of Madagascar, off the east coast of Africa. For the most part, pirates were men. However, there is at least one instance where two women ended up among a pirate crew.

The end of piracy along the Carolina coast was an indication that the two colonies were growing and needed to protect their own trade more than they needed the illegal trade of the pirates. Pirates continue to hold a place of fascination for many who study the history of the time. The reality was one of violent and often ruthless outlaws terrorizing the struggling commerce of the colonies.

5

The Royal Colony of North Carolina

In 1729, King George II and his advisers decided they needed to change the way England's American colonies were governed. They felt the proprietary colonies that had been set up in the 1600s had not worked out to the benefit of the Crown. For the most part, they had not worked out for the proprietors either. When the government approached those holding the eight shares of the Carolina proprietorship, all but one of them agreed to sell their rights back to the Crown. John Carteret, earl Granville, held on to his share.

Granville Tract

John Carteret, earl Granville, had inherited a one-eighth share in Carolina and did not want to give it up in 1729. He was able to strike a deal with the Crown wherein he was allowed to keep a large strip of land along the North Carolina–Virginia border. This strip is referred to as the Granville Tract or Granville District, and it was one of the richest and most densely populated areas in the colony. Politically, it was part of the royal colony of North Carolina. Economically, Lord Granville remained in control of the area. He retained much of the land in the Granville Tract until the state of North Carolina claimed it during the Revolutionary War.

When the Crown and the representatives of the proprietors came to an agreement in 1731, a number of changes took place in North Carolina. These changes were beneficial as people flocked to the area. Over the next 30 years, only Virginia added more people. On the negative side, the change created political turmoil in the colony that continued until independence and the Revolution left the people in charge of their own destiny.

SETTLERS FLOCK TO NORTH CAROLINA

The idea that the government in London, instead of a group of rich men, now controlled the colony gave many the confidence to move to North Carolina. Between 1730 and 1760, the population swelled from approximately 30,000 people to more than 110,000 people. The settlers in North Carolina came from other colonies as well as many places in Europe. There were a few groups that made up a large percentage of these new North Carolinians.

Scotland is located in the northern part of the island of Britain and at times has been an independent country and at other

King George II ruled Ireland and the United Kingdom of England and Scotland from 1727 until 1760. *(Library of Congress, Prints and Photographs Division [LC-USZ62-64702])*

times has been ruled by Great Britain, as it is now. In the 1700s, there were numerous problems in Scotland that made many people willing to move elsewhere. Economic depression in Scotland, coupled with rent increases and evictions for many farmers, contributed to the movement of people out of Scotland. By the middle of the 18th century, the widespread use of an inoculation for smallpox led to population growth in the area, which created even more displaced people.

Almost as soon as the Crown took over North Carolina, Scots began migrating to the area. Anyone who paid for their passage or

Tar Heels

North Carolina's nickname is the Tar Heel State. Although there is no proof of how that name came about, many believe it was a result of the large amount of pine tar that was produced in North Carolina during colonial times. Tar was made by burning the stumps of pine trees and had many applications on board sailing ships. It was used as waterproofing and to help seal seams between planks. It was so prevalent on ships that sailors were often referred to as "tars." One use of pine tar today many people are familiar with is the application of tar to the handle end of baseball bats. This gives players a sticky surface to hold on to and helps keep the bat from slipping in their hands.

the passage of others to America was granted 50 acres by the Crown. Land records in North Carolina show that large amounts of land were granted to Scots at this time. Many of these Scots settled

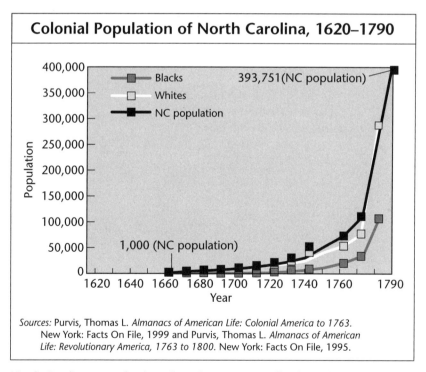

Colonial Population of North Carolina, 1620–1790

- Blacks
- Whites
- NC population

393,751(NC population)

1,000 (NC population)

Population

Year

Sources: Purvis, Thomas L. Almanacs of American Life: Colonial America to 1763. New York: Facts On File, 1999 and Purvis, Thomas L. Almanacs of American Life: Revolutionary America, 1763 to 1800. New York: Facts On File, 1995.

North Carolina grew slowly at first, then grew rapidly after it became a Crown Colony in 1731.

in the Cape Fear area. Reports by travelers of the time state that there were so many Scots in the area, people were more likely to speak Gaelic, the native language of Scotland, than they were to speak English.

The Scots quickly adapted to life in the colonies. Many had left behind stone hovels with dirt floors they shared with their livestock. In North Carolina, they were able to build sturdy wooden houses with chimneys and windows. As they cleared the pine forests of the area, they soon found a ready market for forest products, especially tar and timber used in shipbuilding.

Another large group that came to North Carolina during this time were the Scots-Irish. In 1607, after England defeated the Irish in a war, the king of England, James I, transplanted a large population of Scots from Scotland to the northern part of Ireland known as Ulster. The thinking at the time was that the Scots would take over the area inhabited by the most troublesome of the Irish and turn it into a prosperous area. Although it was not a good situation

Shown in an early 20th-century photograph, this sturdy log cabin near present-day Charlotte, North Carolina, was built around 1726 and is similar to the type of homes many Scots built when they settled in North Carolina. *(Library of Congress, Prints and Photographs Division [HABS, NC,60-___,3-1])*

for the Irish people of the area, as the two sides continue to oppose each other in Northern Ireland today, James I achieved his goal.

By the 18th century, many of the Scots in Ireland had grown dissatisfied with their situation. Landlords had raised rents, and this, along with bad weather, livestock diseases, and crop failures forced many Scots-Irish to consider moving as their ancestors had when they came to Ireland. Most of the early Scots-Irish to arrive in the American colonies ended up in Pennsylvania and Maryland. Some came as indentured servants; others found it increasingly difficult to buy land in those more settled colonies.

A third ethnic group also made it to North Carolina in large numbers. These were people of German descent. They came from different parts of Germany and Switzerland. Some came for the freedom to practice their religion, and others came for the opportunity to purchase their own land. For a long time, there were parts of North Carolina where the majority of the people spoke only German.

Indentured Servants

The cost of getting to North America was often more than many of the people who wanted to come could afford. Almost as soon as people started coming to the American colonies, they brought people with them who were under contract to work for them. They paid for their passage in exchange for a number of years of labor. These contracts were called indentures. The people who worked under them were called indentured servants. Indentures varied in length from three to seven years, and people were often promised cash bonuses for completion of their indentures.

Many of the original settlers who came from Virginia to North Carolina were former indentured servants. Some had completed their period of indenture; others had run away before their time was up. People agreed to become indentured servants because they believed that life would be better for them in the colonies even if they had to be other people's servants for a period of time. Many indentured servants served as agricultural workers, especially in the Chesapeake Bay area. Many died because of the harsh working conditions on plantations. Most of those who managed to live through their indenture could not afford to live in the settled areas of colonies such as Virginia and Maryland. These are the people who came to the backcountry of North Carolina, where land was cheap and people willing to work hard could become successful farmers.

All these people created a number of problems on the frontier of North Carolina. By this time, the Tuscarora had left the area, but the Cherokee still held on to the mountainous western part of the colony. It was just a matter of time before these two groups would clash as the demand for more and more land increased.

SLAVES AND PLANTERS IN NORTH CAROLINA

As the 18th century progressed, the vast majority of people in North Carolina were farmers who worked small farms with their families. This was especially true of the people on the frontier. However, there were also a number of large plantations in North Carolina that supported a privileged group of planters. Some of the largest plantations in North Carolina covered more than 10,000 acres, and there were a few plantations that were five times that size.

Life on these plantations was quite luxurious for the owners and their families. Servants, most of whom were slaves by the middle of the 18th century, did all the work, and the planters and their families lived like the nobility in England. They spent their time in leisure pursuits like hunting and riding. The children of the plantation owners were some of the few people in the colony who received educations. They would often start out with private tutors and then the boys would go off to England to attend Oxford or Cambridge. These people had all the best goods that money could buy. Many of the luxury items that they had were imported from England.

To maintain their lifestyle, plantation owners took numerous Africans who had been forced into slavery. Most of the slaves in North Carolina were imported from Virginia or through Charleston, South Carolina. By 1760, 30 percent of the population of North Carolina, more than 33,000 people, was of African-American descent. Only a very small number of these people were free. The overwhelming majority were slaves, and frequently they were not treated as well as a planter's prize racehorse. Slaves were forced to live in squalid shacks with dirt floors. They were given only the barest necessities of clothing, and many children were forced to go about naked.

Special laws protected the owners of slaves so they could hang on to their property. In the eyes of the law, slaves were often considered like livestock and other property belonging to the planters. Most of the slaves lived in the eastern part of the colony, where the large plantations were. Very few of the small farm owners in the interior could afford or wanted slaves.

As the population and its diversity increased, a number of political tensions arose in North Carolina. First and foremost among them was the conflict between the ideas the Crown had about running its colonies and the customs that had become established under the proprietors. There were also conflicts between the long-established area of Albemarle and the more recently settled country along the Cape Fear River.

ROYAL GOVERNORS AND THE COLONIAL ASSEMBLY

When North Carolina became a royal colony, it fell to the Board of Trade, appointed by the king, to choose a governor for the colony and to make sure the governor adhered to the Crown's new rules for the colonies. The first royal governor of North Carolina was George Burrington, who had been governor once before under the proprietors. He arrived in the colony in February 1731 and almost immediately ran into problems with the assembly.

The people of North Carolina, through their elected assembly, assumed that although the proprietors had been replaced by the Crown, the laws, rules, and practices established under the charter would remain in effect. The governor's instructions from the Crown made it clear that London had no intention of being limited by the charter. The governor set about following his instructions to make changes in North Carolina. The assembly did all they could to prevent the governor from carrying out his orders. They refused to approve any of the changes in taxes and appointments the governor made. When the governor failed to get the cooperation of the assembly, he dismissed it and did what he saw was his job without them for the next two years.

The members of the assembly could not control the governor, who ran the colony like a dictator. Their only option was to complain to London and the Board of Trade. Burrington probably would have remained the governor in spite of the complaints from the colony had he not revealed in his own reports that he was unfit for the job. After three years, the Board of Trade recalled Burrington and sent Gabriel Johnston to replace him in November 1734.

Governor Johnston immediately realized he would have to work with the assembly if he was to succeed as governor. Johnston turned out to be an excellent politician. He was able to keep the assembly involved while he managed to put into place the changes to taxes and other issues that had caused Burrington so much trouble. Johnston remained governor for 18 years during a time North Carolina was growing rapidly.

One situation Johnston had to deal with was the power of the older counties in the Albemarle region. As the majority in the assembly, the Albemarle representatives had arranged it so their counties would have five representatives each. The newer counties in the Cape Fear area and in the interior had only two representatives each. In this way, the Albemarle area maintained control of the assembly.

The Albemarle majority was the group most likely to oppose the governor and his instructions from London. To be able to change the balance of power in the assembly, a new scheme would have to be devised for representation. Each time the governor tried to make the representation more favorable to the newer counties, he was overruled by the Albemarle-controlled assembly. He was finally able to outsmart them in November 1746, by having the assembly meet in Wilmington instead of New Bern. Many of the Albemarle delegates were forced to stay home because of a storm.

During this session of the assembly, the rules were changed so all counties each had two representatives. The people of Albemarle were so upset by the governor's maneuvers that they went ahead and elected five representatives anyway. When the governor refused to accept all the delegates from Albemarle, they left and stayed away from the assembly for seven years. This set off a long investigation in London that was not concluded until after Governor Johnston died in 1752.

It took until October 1754 for a new royal governor, Arthur Dobbs, to arrive in the colony. When he called the assembly together, all the counties were represented. They met in a spirit of

North Carolina's first newspaper, the *North Carolina Gazette,* began publication on November 15, 1751, in New Bern. It is one of more than 2,000 newspapers known to have been published in the colony and later the state. *(North Carolina Museum of History)*

cooperation between the different regions of the colony and with the new governor. Everyone knew that war between the English colonies and the French and their Indian allies was about to begin. In the face of a common enemy, all the factions wanted to work together. However, more than 20 years of dissension in the colony had created a sense of distrust between North Carolina and the Crown that would make North Carolina a willing participant in the independence movement that would lead to the Declaration of Independence in 1776.

THE FRENCH AND INDIAN WAR, 1755–1762

Starting in 1689, France and England went to war four times. For the most part, North Carolina was not directly affected by the first two wars. Some of the privateers in these wars became pirates who caused problems with the shipping along the Carolina coast. Generally, the fighting took place along the border between French Canada and the New England and New York colonies.

In the war known in the colonies as King George's War (1740–48), North Carolina raised four companies of 100 men each. These men joined a large British force in the Caribbean. Their goal was to attack the Spanish settlement at Cartagena, Columbia. Spain was an ally of France, and Cartagena was one of the richest cities in the Caribbean. The attack on Cartagena in April 1741 was a disaster. Almost half the force was lost in the unsuccessful attempt to capture the city. Many of those who were not shot down in battle died of tropical diseases. In the end, 3,600 Americans left for the attack on Cartagena, and fewer than 600 returned.

While some North Carolinians were off fighting and dying in the tropics, Spanish privateers harassed shipping and attacked a number of towns along the North Carolina coast. The Spanish privateers followed in Blackbeard's footsteps and set up a base on Ocracoke Island. From there, they attacked Beaufort and Brunswick. The privateers seemed to be able to do what they wanted until the people of Brunswick decided to fight back in September 1748. They drove the Spaniards back onto their ships, killing 10 of them. Then the larger of the two Spanish ships began firing its cannons into the town. There was little the people could do except take cover.

Then fate stepped in. The larger of the Spanish ships suddenly caught fire and soon exploded as the fire spread to its gunpowder magazine. The ship was completely destroyed. Those aboard the second ship tried to negotiate with the people of Brunswick to get some of their crew back who had been captured. When the two sides were unable to come to terms, the Spanish ship sailed away without returning any of the goods that had been stolen in the raid.

When peace was declared later in 1748, the French in North America used the relative calm to expand their territory into the Ohio River valley and down the Mississippi River to the Gulf of Mexico. Many of the English colonies, especially Virginia and the Carolinas, had claims that extended beyond the Appalachian Mountains. The original Carolana Charter had extended all the way to the Pacific Ocean. The people on the frontiers of Virginia and the Carolinas were already exploring the lands to the west.

The French continued the tradition they had started in New York and New England. They armed friendly Native Americans and encouraged them to attack the English colonial frontiers. By 1755, the English colonies were completely hemmed in to the north and west by French settlements and forts. The first three wars between the two countries had spilled over to the colonies. In the fourth war, the French and Indian War, North America became a major theater of the fighting.

When war broke out in 1755, the French were better prepared and seemed to be winning. There were numerous defeats for the British and American troops in the wilderness of western Pennsylvania. Finally, a new government came to power in London, and William Pitt was in charge of it. He was determined to drive the French out of North America. To do so required a vast commitment of resources over a long period of time, which resulted in a huge debt for the British government.

In North Carolina, plans were made to strengthen defenses along the frontier. Money was appropriated to raise troops to assist the British in fighting the French and their Indian allies. All along the frontier, Native Americans raided farms and small settlements. In some of the western counties, as many as half the people moved east to the relative safety of more populated areas. The Cherokee, who still controlled their traditional homelands in the mountains, were allied with the French and participated in the raids along the borders of their territory.

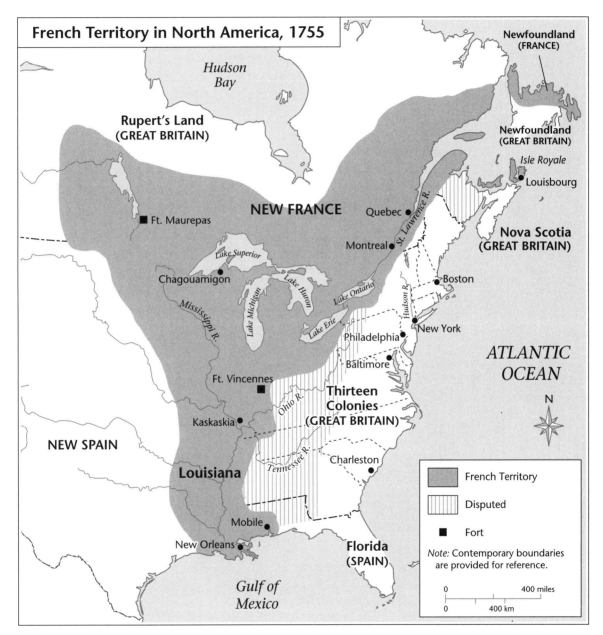

French Territory in North America, 1755

Hudson Bay

Newfoundland (FRANCE)

Rupert's Land (GREAT BRITAIN)

Newfoundland (GREAT BRITAIN)

Isle Royale

Louisbourg

NEW FRANCE

■ Ft. Maurepas

Quebec ●

Montreal ●

St. Lawrence R.

Nova Scotia (GREAT BRITAIN)

Lake Superior

Chagouamigon ●

Lake Michigan

Lake Huron

Lake Ontario

Lake Erie

● Boston

Hudson R.

Mississippi R.

New York ●

Philadelphia ●

Ft. Vincennes ■

Ohio R.

● Baltimore

Thirteen Colonies (GREAT BRITAIN)

ATLANTIC OCEAN

N

NEW SPAIN

Kaskaskia ■

Tennessee R.

● Charleston

Louisiana

Mobile ●

New Orleans ■

Florida (SPAIN)

Gulf of Mexico

French Territory

Disputed

■ Fort

Note: Contemporary boundaries are provided for reference.

0   400 miles

0   400 km

By 1755, the French had expanded their territory into the Ohio River valley and down the Mississippi River to encircle the English colonies.

In 1760 and again in 1761, South Carolina organized attacks that included British regulars and colonial militia against the Cherokee. Militia from North Carolina fought in both campaigns, which had a devastating affect on the Cherokee. In 1761, the combined forces burned 15 Cherokee towns and 1,400 acres of corn crop. In the treaty that ended the fight between the colonies and the Cherokee, the Cherokee were forced to give up more land to the encroaching settlers.

The cooperation between the colonies and the Pitt government in London did not last long. When it came time to pay for the war, London turned to the colonies as a source of revenue. Many people in America rebelled at the idea of Parliament passing direct taxes on the colonies that were not represented in London. In just 12 years, the British and their American colonies would go from fighting together against the French to fighting each other.

6

The Road to Revolution

In the time between the end of the French and Indian War in 1762 and the first armed conflict between British troops and the colonial militia at the Battle of Lexington and Concord (Massachusetts) on April 19, 1775, North Carolina was marked by division. The colony was divided in two different ways. First, the wealthy planters in the eastern half of the colony were pitted against the farmers of the west. The colony was also divided between those who remained loyal to the Crown and those who became increasingly upset with the way the Crown and Parliament were trying to tax and control the colonies. As the Revolution approached, there were no clear lines between the two. Members of the eastern plantation-owning elite became supporters of the Revolution. On the other hand, there were those among the rebellious westerners who ended up supporting Britain and the king. The opposite was also true.

The two divisions did share one common thread. In the internal struggle, those in the western part of the colony protested and even fought for the right to have fair and equal representation in the colonial assembly. When it came to opposing the Crown, there was a similar debate about the lack of representation by the colonies in Parliament. The Revolutionary War eventually solved both problems and brought true democracy to North Carolina.

EAST VERSUS WEST

In the years prior to the Revolution, North Carolina grew rapidly. The eastern half of the colony had been settled first and was home to most of the large plantations in the colony. The wealthy planters had long fought to hang on to a majority control of the colonial assembly. At first they did this by allowing the older counties more representatives than the newer ones in the west. When equal representation for the counties was forced on them, they continued to maintain a majority in the assembly by dividing the eastern half of the colony into more and more counties.

The western part of the colony soon had a larger population than the east. But, since the eastern-controlled assembly was in charge of creating new counties, they were slow to do so for the west. When they did create new counties in the interior, they made sure that there were never more there than in the east. By 1771, the situation had become so inequitable that a representative to the assembly from the western part of the colony represented approximately 7,300 people. In the east, where the population had not grown, the division into smaller and smaller counties had created a situation where each assembly member from the eastern countries represented only about 1,700 people.

Looking back, it can be easily understood why the people in the west wished to regulate the number of representatives so they would be represented in a more equitable manner. As the movement to regulate representation to the assembly grew, those in the west who wanted the system changed became known as Regulators. The part of the problem that upset the people in the west the most was the way the assembly used its power and appointed only easterners to positions within the government. All the judges and sheriffs in the west were people from the eastern part of the colony who used their positions to collect fees that many Regulators felt were unfair.

Numerous accusations were made that officials from the east were using their appointed positions to extort money from the struggling farmers of the west. One of the supposedly worst offenders was Colonel Edmund Fanning, a personal friend of Governor William Tryon, who had moved to North Carolina from New York to accept a number of positions in Orange County. Fanning's abuses of power were considered so severe that Hillsborough, the

The Governor's Palace

While the Regulators organized their resistance to the governor, Tryon decided it was time to settle the colonial capital in one place. Before 1767, the assembly had met in Edenton, New Bern, Wilmington, and Bath. Under the governor's guidance, New Bern was selected as the best location, as it was about halfway between the northern and southern ends of the colony. The only problem was that it was near the coast and a long way from where most of the people in the colony now lived.

If the location was not bad enough, in November 1766, it was decided that an elaborate building should be built to serve as the residence for the governor and the meeting place of the assembly. A builder was brought from England to design an ornate building that was 87 feet wide and 59 feet deep. This two-story building was connected to two wings by a series of columns. At first, the assembly appropriated £5,000 for its construction. When this turned out not to be enough, they appropriated another £10,000. There was not enough money in the colony's accounts to pay this, so a special poll tax on all the residents of the colony was approved. In the end, the underrepresented, poorer people in the more populated west paid for what they called "Tryon's Palace." It was considered one of the most impressive government buildings in English North America when it was completed in 1770.

county seat of Orange county, became the focal point of the conflict between the Regulators and the eastern establishment.

Fanning's abuses and the governor's new place brought the situation to a head. In September 1770, the Regulators took over the courthouse in Hillsborough. In the process, they injured many colonial officials and ruined their private property. When the news of the "Hillsborough Riot" reached the governor, he called out the militia, made up of people mostly from the eastern counties. In the spring of 1771, Governor Tryon led 1,400 militia west. On May 16, 1771, they reached Great Alamance Creek just west of Hillsborough. Here they were met by 2,000 Regulators, about half of whom were armed.

The Regulators requested a meeting with the governor. Tryon refused and gave them an hour to surrender their weapons. The Regulators assumed the governor would give in and waited for the deadline. When the hour was up, the governor ordered the militia

Daniel Boone
(1734–1820)

Daniel Boone was born near Reading, Pennsylvania, in 1734. His parents were Quakers but had some disagreements with their church and left Pennsylvania for the frontier of North Carolina in 1750. In North Carolina, Daniel Boone quickly learned and excelled at the skills needed to be a frontiersman. He became an excellent marksman with both a rifle and bow and arrow. In 1755, he participated in a campaign against the French in the wilderness of the Ohio River valley.

Starting in 1767, Boone made many trips over the mountains into what would become Tennessee and Kentucky. He was one of a group of men known as Long Hunters who went alone or in small groups far into the western territory, hunting and trapping. In 1775, he established a fort that was known as Boonesborough. He also helped lay out the Wilderness Road through the Cumberland Gap, which allowed many people to move westward after the Revolution. As settlement caught up with Boone, he continued to move westward and finally settled near what is now St. Louis, Missouri, where he died in 1820.

In this partial late 19th-century image, Daniel Boone protects his family from a Native American. *(Library of Congress, Prints and Photographs Division [LC-USZC2-3756])*

to fire. It appears that the Regulators were not the only ones who thought the governor was bluffing, because at first, the militia failed to fire. When the governor repeated his orders, they opened fire.

The Regulators fired back and approximately nine men on each side were killed. Many more were wounded—more than 60 among the militia and an unknown number of Regulators. Twelve of the Regulator leaders were arrested, tried, and convicted of treason. The governor pardoned six of them. The other six were hanged. After the hangings, the governor offered pardons to any of the Regulators who acknowledged the authority of the governor.

Approximately 6,500 Regulators are known to have accepted the pardons. At the same time, 1,500 Regulator families left the colony rather than give in to the governor. Many of them are believed to have crossed the mountains into what is now Kentucky and Tennessee. This was still an unsettled area that had been explored by a number of adventurous North Carolinians, including Daniel Boone.

THE SUGAR ACT,
April 5, 1764

After the French and Indian War, Great Britain was faced with a huge debt. Many in the English government felt the American colonies should share the burden of paying that debt. The Crown had also decided to keep a force of 10,000 regular soldiers in North America. The colonies were expected to pay for that as well. The first attempt to increase revenue from the colonies was known as the Sugar Act and it became law on April 5, 1764.

It was intended to eliminate the illegal trade that had grown up between the English colonies in North America and the non-British sugar producers in the Carribean. It also included a duty on legally imported sugar. The trade and tariff parts of the Sugar Act had little or no impact on the the people of North Carolina. In New England, where the sugar trade was a major part of the economy, there were a number of protests over the bill.

The Sugar Act also made a number of changes in the way taxes were collected in the colonies. It strengthened the authority of the customs inspectors. More important, it set up a vice-admiralty court in Halifax, Nova Scotia, that was responsible for hearing all smuggling and customs-related cases. Before this, local courts had juries made up of the friends, neighbors, and others who had an interest in the illegal trade. The Crown officials found it all but impossible to get convictions with juries sympathetic to the ship captains and merchants who were brought before them.

THE STAMP ACT,
March 22, 1765

The Sugar Act was just the first step in getting revenue from the colonies. The next step was a direct tax. On March 22, 1765, Parliament passed the Stamp Act, which more than any other single action set Britain and its colonies on the path that would lead to war. The Stamp Act was scheduled to go into effect on November 1, 1765. After the date, all legal transactions, licenses, printed materials, diplomas, ships' papers, playing cards, and a number of other items would need to have a stamp attached to them.

When affixed to goods, this stamp signified that a tax must be paid upon purchase. Many colonists felt that the British unfairly introduced these taxes when they implemented the Stamp Act in 1765, which affected goods ranging from business transactions to playing cards. *(Library of Congress, Prints and Photographs Division [LC-USZ61-539])*

The idea of the Stamp Act was not the problem. Stamp taxes were common in England, and some of the colonies had used them in the past. This type of tax is still used extensively in the United States, although the actual stamps are rarely placed on goods anymore. When news of the Stamp Act reached the colonies, there was a widespread and at times violent reaction to the bill. People objected because Parliament had decided to tax them directly even though the colonies had no representation there. The idea of "No taxation without representation" became one of the rallying points for colonists opposed to British authority. Throughout the colonies, people organized into groups known as the Sons of Liberty to protest the Act.

There was a strong reaction to the Stamp Act in North Carolina. The speaker of the assembly, John Ashe, was one of the leaders of the opposition to the Stamp Act. He reportedly told Governor Tryon, "We will

Sons of Liberty

When the Stamp Act was passed by Parliament in 1765, people in the colonies formed groups in their communities to protest the act. One of the few opponents of the Stamp Act in Parliament's House of Commons, Isaac Barré, called the protestors the "sons of liberty." Soon the name spread to the colonies, where it was readily adopted. It was the various Sons of Liberty groups that held "tea parties" in Boston, New Jersey, and South Carolina when the Tea Act was passed. The Sons of Liberty were also responsible for forming the Committees of Correspondence that kept the Patriots throughout the colonies current on what was occurring. The letters passed between these local committees are credited with bringing about the First Continental Congress.

resist it to the death." In the Wilmington area, Ashe, along with Hugh Waddell, Abner Nash, Robert Howe, and others formed the Sons of Liberty. Other groups were started throughout the state.

Colonists denounce the Stamp Act in 1765. *(Library of Congress)*

On October 19, 1765, the Sons of Liberty led a demonstration of 500 people through the streets of Wilmington. It is said that they chanted, "Liberty, property, and no stamp duty." In front of the Wilmington courthouse, they hung a dummy dressed like a British official and then threw it onto their bonfire. On November 16, another protest confronted Dr. William Houston, who had been appointed North Carolina's stamp agent. Faced with 400 angry demonstrators, Dr. Houston decided it would be best to resign as stamp agent.

No stamps were being issued for fear the situation would become violent. Although some business continued illegally without stamps, shipping and the courts were at a standstill. In January 1766, a serious problem arose when two merchant ships, the *Dobbs* and the *Patience*, tried to leave Brunswick, North Carolina, without stamps on their papers.

The British ship *Viper* seized the two merchant vessels, and the colony reached a crisis. Some felt Captain Jacob Lobb of the *Viper* was wrong to seize the ships because there were no stamps available. British officials in the colony wanted the ships sent to the vice-admiralty court in Halifax, where they would then be forfeited.

On February 18, 1766, a meeting was held in Wilmington, and an Association Against the Stamp Act was formed. The next day, a large force of armed Patriots surrounded the governor's house. They quarreled with the governor, then broke into the office of the tax collector and took back the papers of the seized ships. On February 20, the mob returned and requested the resignation of certain colonial officials. William Pennington, who was the colony's comptroller, joined the crowd and took an oath to resist the Stamp Act.

On March 18, 1766, the king signed a bill passed in Parliament repealing the Stamp Act. It appeared that the colonists had won the debate over "no taxation without representation." However, attached to the bill repealing the Stamp Act was something called the Declaratory Resolution. This resolution made it clear that Parliament still believed they had the right to pass whatever laws they thought necessary to govern the colonies. It also stated they had the right to use whatever force was necessary to make the colonies comply.

TOWNSHEND DUTIES,
June 29, 1767

A little more than a year after the Stamp Act had been repealed, Parliament used the authority of the Declaratory Resolution to once again try to raise tax revenue in the colonies. One of the major points people like Benjamin Franklin had made to Parliament was that the Stamp Act was a direct tax on the people of the colonies. He, and others, stated that direct taxes were wrong when the people being taxed had no representatives in Parliament. In 1767, Parliament tried a different approach. They passed a number of indirect taxes on certain goods that were imported into the colonies. This type of tax is called a duty. As a group, they were called the Townshend Duties after Charles Townshend, the king's official who devised them.

The Townshend Duties were imposed on lead, glass, paper, painter's colors, wine, and tea. At first, the people in the colonies did not know how to react to the Townshend Duties. Radical leaders in Massachusetts and Virginia took the lead. They suggested that the people of the colonies join together and refuse to import and/or buy any goods from Britain. The non-importation movement took a while to build a following, but eventually many people in all the colonies agreed to boycott British goods.

In North Carolina, on November 2, 1769, the assembly voted unanimously to support a nonimportation policy. Similar agreements had been reached by this time in most of the colonies. Although dissent was again peaceful in North Carolina, violence broke out elsewhere. On January 18, 1770, British soldiers and Patriots clashed in New York in what was called the Battle of Golden Hill. This was more of a brawl than an actual battle. No one was killed, but numerous people on both sides were injured. In Boston, it was a different story. On March 5, 1770, British soldiers opened fire on a crowd of protesters who had thrown snowballs at them. This event is known as the Boston Massacre; five Patriots were killed and six others were seriously wounded.

Parliament once again realized that their plan to tax the colonies was not going to succeed. In April 1770, Parliament

Paul Revere's engraving of the Boston Massacre depicts the event that many consider the beginning of the struggle for independence. It occurred on March 5, 1770. *(Library of Congress, Prints and Photographs Division [LC-USZ62-35522])*

repealed all the Townshend Duties except for the one on tea. The duty on tea was kept primarily because Parliament still believed it had the right to tax the colonies and wanted to prove it. With the repeal of the Townshend Duties, it appeared that the problems with the colonies had subsided. A period of relative quiet followed until Parliament stepped in to try and save the struggling British East India Company.

TEA ACT,
May 10, 1773

In 1773, it looked like the long-established British trading company, the British East India Company, was going to go bankrupt. Under early laws, all the tea shipped from the Far East by the company had to be sent to England, where duties were paid and the tea was sold to importers. The price was then marked up to provide a profit for the importers. The importers then shipped the tea to the colonies, where another duty was paid and the colonial tea merchants added their profit margin.

The Tea Act of 1773 made it legal for the East India Company to ship tea directly to the American colonies without going through the middlemen and added duties in England. The bill would have actually made British tea cheaper in the colonies. However, it gave the East India Company a monopoly and made it illegal for the colonies to import tea from anywhere else. At the time, much of the tea in the colonies was smuggled in from Dutch sources in the Caribbean and elsewhere.

After the first shipment of tea arrived in Boston, the Sons of Liberty, disguised as Native Americans, boarded the ships on December 16, 1773, and dumped £10,000 worth of tea in Boston Harbor. This is called the Boston Tea Party, and similar events took place in other colonies as well. In North Carolina, support for resistance to the Tea Act was done differently.

On October 25, 1774, 51 women from a number of counties met in Edenton, North Carolina, for a tea party. However, these Patriot women did not come together to drink tea. They gathered to show their support for a boycott of British tea and other goods. The women at North Carolina's first tea party promised not to drink any British tea or wear clothes imported from England. In March 1775, another group of patriotic women gathered in Wilmington, North Carolina. They went one step further than the women in Edenton. In addition to pledging to follow the boycott of British goods, they burned some tea as well. The North Carolina Tea Parties are considered the first organized participation by women in the protest movement in the colonies.

In this illustration published in London in 1775 that makes fun of the colonists' efforts to boycott tea, American women in Edenton, North Carolina, vow not to engage in that "pernicious custom of drinking tea." *(Library of Congress, Prints and Photographs Division [LC-USZ62-12711])*

Committees of Correspondence

In the 18th century, it was difficult to communicate ideas and information over long distances. There were very few newspapers in the colonies and none of the electronic media that people depend on today existed. The Boston, Massachusetts, town meeting decided in 1772 to set up a committee that would "state the Rights of the Colonists" and share them with other communities in Massachusetts. The Committee of Correspondence worked so well that the idea soon spread to all the colonies. It was through the Committees of Correspondence that the call for the First Continental Congress went out.

At this point, most of the people in the colonies wanted to resolve their problems with the Crown. Only a few of the most radical Patriots were talking about independence. However, the reaction to the Boston Tea Party by the Crown helped push the colonies down the road to revolution.

THE INTOLERABLE ACTS, 1774

After the Boston Tea Party, Parliament decided to force the colonies to do as Parliament instructed. In 1774, they passed a series of laws known as the Coercive Acts. In the colonies, they were called the Intolerable Acts. There were a number of provisions that were intended to bring the colonies under control. They included closing the port of Boston until the tea that had been dumped in the harbor was paid for. In reaction to the Intolerable Acts, North Carolina and many other colonies created assemblies that met outside the influence of the royal governors and other Crown officials.

Through these provincial assemblies and the Committees of Correspondence that were formed, the colonies agreed to send representatives to Philadelphia to meet as a Continental Congress. North Carolina's First Provincial Congress met and agreed to send William Hooper, Joseph Hewes, and Richard Caswell to the First Continental Congress. Although the hope of many was that the colonies and the Crown could reconcile their differences, war and independence were not far away.

7

The War of Independence

THE FIRST CONTINENTAL CONGRESS,
September 5 to October 26, 1774

When the delegates came together in Philadelphia in fall 1774, they were still intent on trying to reconcile with the Crown and Parliament. They sent a list of complaints and resolutions to the king. Their plan called for increasing the boycott of British goods. If that did not work, the next step was to stop all exports from the colonies to Britain. They were declaring economic warfare on Britain.

The delegates planned to return to Philadelphia in 1775 to decide on their next step. On April 19, 1775, the British forces in Boston marched inland to Lexington and Concord, Massachusetts, to arrest Patriot leaders John Hancock and Samuel Adams. They also planned to confiscate a stash of Patriot weapons in Concord. Adams and Hancock avoided capture, and the battles that took place changed the situation from an economic war to one of fighting and killing.

THE WAR STARTS IN NORTH CAROLINA

After Lexington and Concord, the Provincial Congress of North Carolina became the working government. In May 1775, the royal governor, Josiah Martin, took refuge at Fort Johnston at the

The Battle of Lexington and Concord
(April 19, 1775)

On April 14, 1775, General Thomas Gage, the British commander in Boston, was given orders to use force against the rebellious Patriots of Massachusetts. He immediately made plans to go on the offensive. Eight hundred British soldiers, who were called redcoats by the Patriots because of their scarlet uniforms, were sent to capture Patriot leaders and supplies in Lexington and Concord about 20 miles west of Boston. Thanks to Paul Revere and other members of the Boston Sons of Liberty who rode out to spread the alarm, the Patriot militia in Lexington and Concord were forewarned.

When the British arrived at Lexington, there were 70 Patriots lined up on the town common to meet them. The British ordered the Patriots to lay down their weapons. Instead, the Patriots tried to get away and the British opened fire. Eight colonists were killed, and another 10 were wounded.

When the British marched on to Concord, they were met by a much larger Patriot force and were forced to turn around at the North Bridge. The Patriots harassed the redcoats as they retreated to Boston. Along the way, almost 300 British soldiers were killed or wounded. The Patriots lost fewer than 100. The Revolution had started.

Now on the National Register of Historic Places, Fort Johnston is located in Southport, at the mouth of the Cape Fear River. Governor Martin took refuge in the British-held fort briefly at the start of the Revolutionary War. *(Library of Congress, Prints and Photographs Division [HABS, NC, 10-SOUPO,2-1])*

mouth of the Cape Fear River. The fort was still held by British troops. When North Carolina Patriots attacked and burned the fort, Governor Martin moved onto a British ship. He was the first royal governor to be forced out of the colonies.

From aboard ship, Governor Martin planned to teach the Patriots of North Carolina a lesson. As in most colonies, many people in North Carolina disagreed with the Patriots and wanted to remain loyal to the Crown. They were called Loyalists or Tories. The governor planned to create a large army of Loyalists and combine them with a force of British regulars to regain control of the colony.

Once his plan was approved by his superiors, Martin sent word to the Loyalists in North Carolina to come together near what is now Fayetteville, North Carolina. By the beginning of 1776, there

The Mecklenburg Declaration of Independence
(May 20, 1775)

On the flag and state seal of North Carolina is the date May 20, 1775. On this date, Patriots met in Mecklenburg County, North Carolina, and many believe that the members at that meeting drew up and signed a declaration of independence. The secretary of the meeting was John McNitt Alexander, and he reportedly made five copies of the Mecklenburg Declaration and may have forwarded one to the North Carolina delegation to the Continental Congress. However, on September 3, 1800, a fire at Alexander's house destroyed the remaining copies and all other records from the meeting. No original copies of the Mecklenburg Declaration have been found.

Alexander then tried to create a new copy from memory. There were numerous errors in the copy that brought the legiti-macy of the Mecklenburg Declaration into question. Some of the wording of the copy was very close to the Declaration of Independence passed at the Second Continental Congress on July 4, 1776. Some have accused Alexander of plagiarism for trying to pass off parts of the actual Declaration as belonging to the Mecklenburg one. It seems unlikely that Thomas Jefferson stole from a copy of the Mecklenburg Declaration. Unless an original of the Mecklenburg Declaration is found and verified, the controversy will continue.

There is no doubt that there was a meeting on May 20, 1775, in Mecklenburg County, where people expressed their support for the Patriots in Massachusetts. They undoubtedly also expressed their dissatisfaction with the Crown and Governor Martin.

Loyalists, Patriots, and Undecideds

By the time fighting began in the colonies, the people were equally divided into three groups. The Patriots were ready and willing to fight for their rights and eventually for independence. The second group was made up of the Loyalists, who were loyal to the king and wanted to remain British subjects. The final third were people who had yet to choose a side.

were 1,500 Loyalists gathered and ready to fight. Their objective was to seize Wilmington, which was the center of Patriot activity. In February, 1,100 Patriots led by Colonels Richard Caswell and Alexander Lillington heard the Loyalists were on the move.

To reach Wilmington, the Loyalists would have to cross Moore's Creek Bridge. On February 27, 1776, the Patriot force hid in the woods around the bridge and waited for the Loyalists. When the Loyalists began crossing the bridge, the Patriots opened fire. In

The Battle of Moore's Creek was the first Revolutionary War battle fought in North Carolina. The area where it was fought, shown in this photograph, is now protected by the National Park Service. *(National Park Service)*

the first minutes of the battle, 50 Loyalists were killed. The rest of the Loyalists tried to flee. Some got away, but 850 of them were captured along with 2,000 weapons. The Battle of Moores Creek was North Carolina's first battle of the Revolution. It would not be its last.

THE SECOND CONTINENTAL CONGRESS

When the delegates came together for the Second Continental Congress in 1776, the idea of reevaluating their economic sanctions was a thing of the past. It was time to discuss declaring independence from Britain. There was still resistance to the idea in many corners. In North Carolina, in April 1776, the Fourth Provincial Congress met and voted to give their support to the idea of independence.

On April 12, 1776, North Carolina's Fourth Provincial Congress voted unanimously to accept the Halifax Resolves, which instructed their delegates to the Continental Congress to support any efforts at independence by the colonies. After much debate, Thomas Jefferson put the thoughts of many in the Continental Congress into words, and the Declaration of Independence was drafted.

On July 4, 1776, the delegates to the Second Continental Congress voted unanimously to adopt the Declaration of Independence. William Hooper, Joseph Hewes, and John Penn of North Carolina, along with delegates from the other colonies, signed the

The First Paragraph of the Declaration of Independence

"When in the Course of human events, it becomes necessary for one people to dissolve the political bands which have connected them with another, and to assume among the Powers of the earth, the separate and equal station to which the Laws of Nature and of Nature's God entitle them, a decent respect to the opinions of mankind requires that they should declare the causes which impel them to the separation."

William Hooper signed the Declaration of Independence on behalf of North Carolina. *(Library of Congress, Prints and Photographs Division [LC-USZ62-64708])*

document, and the United States was created. However, it would take a long and bloody war with Britain to ensure that independence was achieved. In the next seven years, more than 20,000 soldiers from North Carolina fought against the British at various times throughout the colonies.

The Second Continental Congress became the unifying authority for the united colonies in their struggle with the British and remained in session throughout the war. Other than the fact that the colonies sent their delegates to the Congress, they had no official status. In 1777, the Congress passed the Articles of Confederation, which bound the states into a loose confederation. However, the Articles were not officially adopted until 1781. Meanwhile, the war continued, first in the North and then the South.

THE WAR IN THE NORTH

George Washington led the newly formed Continental army in the siege of Boston that included the Battle of Bunker Hill in June 1775. In March 1776, the arrival of cannons in Boston gave Washington the advantage, and the British evacuated the city. The war then moved to New York, where the British repeatedly defeated the Patriot forces, forcing them to flee to New Jersey and Pennsylvania. For a period of time, the war remained a stalemate in the North. Eventually, the Americans gained the upper hand and the British decided to turn their attentions to the South.

THE WAR IN THE SOUTH

The British first gained control of Georgia in 1778. After a failed attempt to liberate Savannah by a combined force of French naval, army, and Patriot forces in January 1779, the British headed north into the Carolinas. The Siege of Charleston (South Carolina) began in February 1780. When the city finally fell to the British on May 12, 1780, it was the worst defeat of the Revolution for the Patriots. Five thousand Continental soldiers were captured, and 1,500 of them were from North Carolina. With Savannah and Charleston under British control, the Patriots were on the defensive and continued to be driven north through South Carolina and into North Carolina. The objective of the British commanding general, Charles, Lord Cornwallis, was to take the war to Virginia, which he considered the center of radical thought in the Americas.

THE WAR IN NORTH CAROLINA

As the British successes in Georgia and South Carolina became known in North Carolina, the Loyalists in the area took action. For two years, starting in the middle of 1780, North Carolina was in a

The Patriots secured an important victory against the Loyalists at the Battle of King's Mountain. This engraving of the battlefield appeared in Benson Lossing's *The Pictorial Field-Book of the Revolution.* (*North Carolina Museum of History*)

state of civil war. Bands of Loyalists and Patriots roamed the state, attacking the homes and farms of people they believed to be on the opposite side. This fighting of neighbor against neighbor led to a number of problems for the Loyalists who tried to stay in the United States after the war.

Cornwallis in the meantime had left Charleston. On August 16, 1780, the Patriots suffered another defeat at the Battle of Camden (South Carolina). Nine hundred Patriots died at Camden. Approximately half of them were from North Carolina. After Camden, the Patriots poured more resources into the South and were able to put together victories against segments of Cornwallis's forces at the Battle of King's Mountain on October 7, 1780, and the Battle of Cowpens on January 7, 1781. Both of these battles were fought in South Carolina close to the North Carolina border.

Despite his losses, Cornwallis continued north. On March 15, 1781, he reached Guilford Courthouse, near present-day Greensboro, North Carolina. Waiting for the British at Guilford Courthouse were more than 4,000 Continental soldiers and state militia. Cornwallis had only about 1,900 men, but he figured his war-tested troops could handle the Patriots, especially the militia units, many of whom had never been in a battle.

The Continental Army and the Militia

Although the combined population of the colonies had risen to 2.5 million people, keeping a sufficient force in the field was an ongoing problem for American military leaders. Troops recruited into the Continental army often had to serve for only a year. At the end of their term of service, the soldiers would often pack up and go home, even if there was a battle about to be fought. Also, the Continental Congress had no authority to raise money and found it difficult to pay its army.

Every state also had militia units that could be called up at any time to deal with local situations. At times, militia units that were usually poorly trained and ill-equipped were put into the front lines to face seasoned British troops. The Americans never had more than 20,000 troops in the field at one time during the war. They could have brought the war to an end much sooner if they had been able to recruit, train, and equip a more professional army.

General Nathaniel Greene was in charge of the American forces and arranged them in three lines. Greene's first line consisted of militia, including the North Carolinians. They were backed by a company of riflemen from Virginia. The third line consisted of more experienced Continental troops with units from Virginia and Maryland.

The terrain favored the Americans, as there were woods and brush to provide cover, which made it difficult for the British to advance in their usual tightly formed lines. The North Carolinians and other militia units in the first line did better than expected. They were able to inflict heavy casualties on the Redcoats before they were forced to fall back to the second line. Again the British came under heavy fire. Losing many soldiers, the British broke the second line as well.

Greene expected his third line to hold. However, they too were forced into retreat. The British appeared to have won the only major battle fought in North Carolina. But when the tally was made, the British had lost over a quarter of their force—532 British soldiers were reported dead or wounded. The Americans suffered only 78 killed and 183 wounded. Cornwallis reportedly said, "The Americans fought like demons." When news of the battle reached London, one member of Parliament stated, "Another such victory would ruin the British Army."

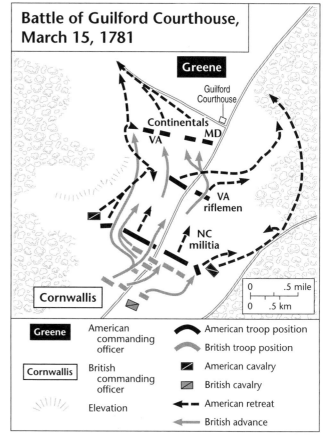

Although the British won the battle, their losses were much greater than those of the Americans. British losses helped bring the war to an end.

THE END OF THE REVOLUTION

By the time Cornwallis reached Virginia, many in England had decided to give up the colonies. At first, Cornwallis was able to operate successfully in Virginia. However, the American forces from throughout the colonies headed to Virginia in hopes of defeating Cornwallis and bringing the war to an end. In addition, the French had entered the war on the side of the Americans and had positioned a large fleet off the Virginia coast, cutting off any chance for reinforcements to reach Cornwallis.

Washington had been preparing to attack New York, which the British had held since 1776. Instead, he turned his troops south. By October 1781, 16,000 American and French troops had Cornwallis and about 8,000 men surrounded at Yorktown, Virginia. During the first week of October, the American troops began digging trenches that would let them approach the British lines. At the same time, they began bombarding the British position. By October 17, 1781, Cornwallis had had enough and surrendered. Two days later, on October 19, 1781, the British troops lined up and officially surrendered to George Washington. The war was over, and the 13 British colonies were now an independent country, but it would be a number of years before they would become the United States.

8

Becoming Part
of a Nation

By the end of 1776, the North Carolina had drafted and adopted a new state constitution. Richard Caswell, who had been a delegate to both the First and Second Continental Congresses and a militia colonel at the Battle of Moore's Creek Bridge, was elected the first governor of the state of North Carolina. Many other states were quick to draft new constitutions as well.

However, the people of the 13 states were extremely reluctant to give power to a central government. They were in the middle of a war to overthrow what they thought of as the tyranny of the Crown and Parliament. They were not going to give up one tyrant for another, even if it was one of their own making. During the Revolution, the Continental Congress came up with the Articles of Confederation to bring the 13 states loosely together. As soon as the war was over, if not before, there were problems with the Articles of Confederation.

ARTICLES OF CONFEDERATION

The Second Continental Congress was raising an army and directing the war efforts of the nation, but it had no real authority. In June 1776, the Congress created a committee to come up with a plan for a federal government. John Dickinson of Pennsylvania chaired the committee that came up with a plan for a fairly strong central government. When the plan was presented to the Congress,

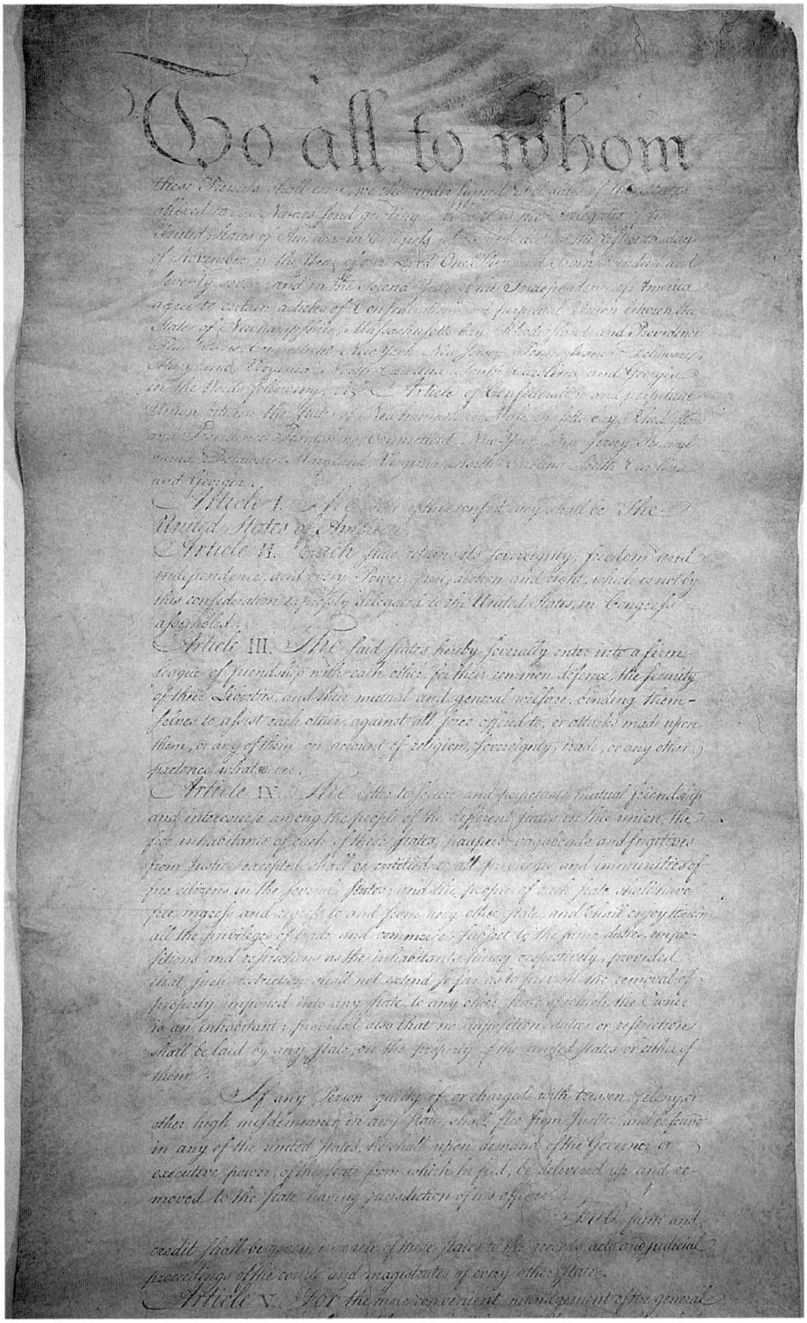

The Articles of Confederation, shown here, were written by a committee of the Continental Congress and intended as a constitution for the colonies.
(National Archives, National Archives Building [NWCTB-360-MISC-ROLL10F81])

it quickly became apparent that many of the delegates would not support it.

Each colony had come about through an almost unique set of circumstances, and the people identified with their respective colonies. People in North Carolina were loyal to their state but really had no sense of a national identity. The same was true in most of the colonies. As a compromise, the Articles of Confederation were drawn up and sent to the states in 1777 for approval. All the states had to agree in order for the articles to become the law of the land.

A number of problems arose during the ratification process. One of the problems had to do with the lands to the west of the Appalachian Mountains. States such as the Carolinas, Virginia, and New York claimed lands to the west. The original charter for the Carolinas had granted a strip of land that ran from the Atlantic to the Pacific Ocean. When New York and Virginia agreed to cede their claims to western lands to the federal government, Maryland finally became the last state to ratify the Articles of Confederation in 1781.

By the time the Treaty of Paris, which settled many of the differences between the new United States and Britain, was finally signed in 1783, more problems had developed with the Articles of Confederation. The federal government was having trouble paying its debts. It had no source of income and had to ask the states for money. Most states only gave the federal government a small portion of what was needed to meet the government's obligations. As a result, some of the soldiers who served in the Revolution did not receive their full pay.

Many of the states experienced economic hard times as the former colonies adjusted to their new status as part of an independent country. Personal debt was soon as big a problem as public debt. Those who had borrowed heavily to rebuild their farms and plantations after the war were having trouble repaying their loans. After the war, there was a general depression in the economy throughout the new United States. In Massachusetts, in 1786 and 1787 a group of farmers protested against problems caused by mounting debt. This has come to be known as Shays's Rebellion. There was no organized rebellion in North Carolina, but the people of the state experienced hard times.

The British and the newly independent United States finally compromised when they signed the Treaty of Paris of 1783, two years after the fighting had stopped in the colonies. *(Library of Congress, Prints and Photographs Division [LC-USZ6-279])*

By 1786, a number of problems between the states had developed, and some of the states sent representatives to a convention in Annapolis, Maryland. The intent of the Annapolis Convention was to consider a federal plan to regulate trade. Only five states—Virginia, Delaware, New York, Pennsylvania, and New Jersey—sent delegates. The delegates quickly realized they had two problems. One was the lack of attendance by the states, and the other was the limitations of the Articles of Confederation.

The delegates to the Annapolis Convention, led by Alexander Hamilton, sent out a call for a convention to be held the following year in Philadelphia. The idea of the convention was to amend the Articles of Confederation to solve some of the problems being faced by the states.

THE CONSTITUTIONAL CONVENTION, 1787

When the delegates convened in Philadelphia in May 1787, they quickly decided that the Articles of Confederation needed to be scrapped and a new document organizing the federal government needed to be drawn up. The delegates of all the states except Rhode Island, which did not send any delegates, began the process of writing a new constitution. The list of delegates included many well-known Patriot leaders. George Washington was elected to serve as president of the Convention. North Carolina sent William Blount, Hugh Williamson, and Richard D. Spaight to represent the state.

Hugh Williamson represented North Carolina at the Constitutional Convention and worked diligently for the state's ratification of the Constitution. *(National Archives)*

There were many controversies surrounding the writing of the Constitution. The delegates had to compromise on many issues and balance the desire of the states to control their own affairs and the need for a federal government to unite and lead the country. One major hurdle was the way the states would be represented in the national congress. Large states such as Massachusetts and Virginia wanted representation to be based on population. Small states wanted every state to have equal representation. Eventually what is known as the Great Compromise was reached.

Preamble to the U.S. Constitution

"We the People of the United States, in Order to form a more perfect Union, establish Justice, insure domestic Tranquility, provide for the common defence, promote the general Welfare, and secure the Blessings of Liberty to ourselves and our Posterity, do ordain and establish this Constitution for the United States of America."

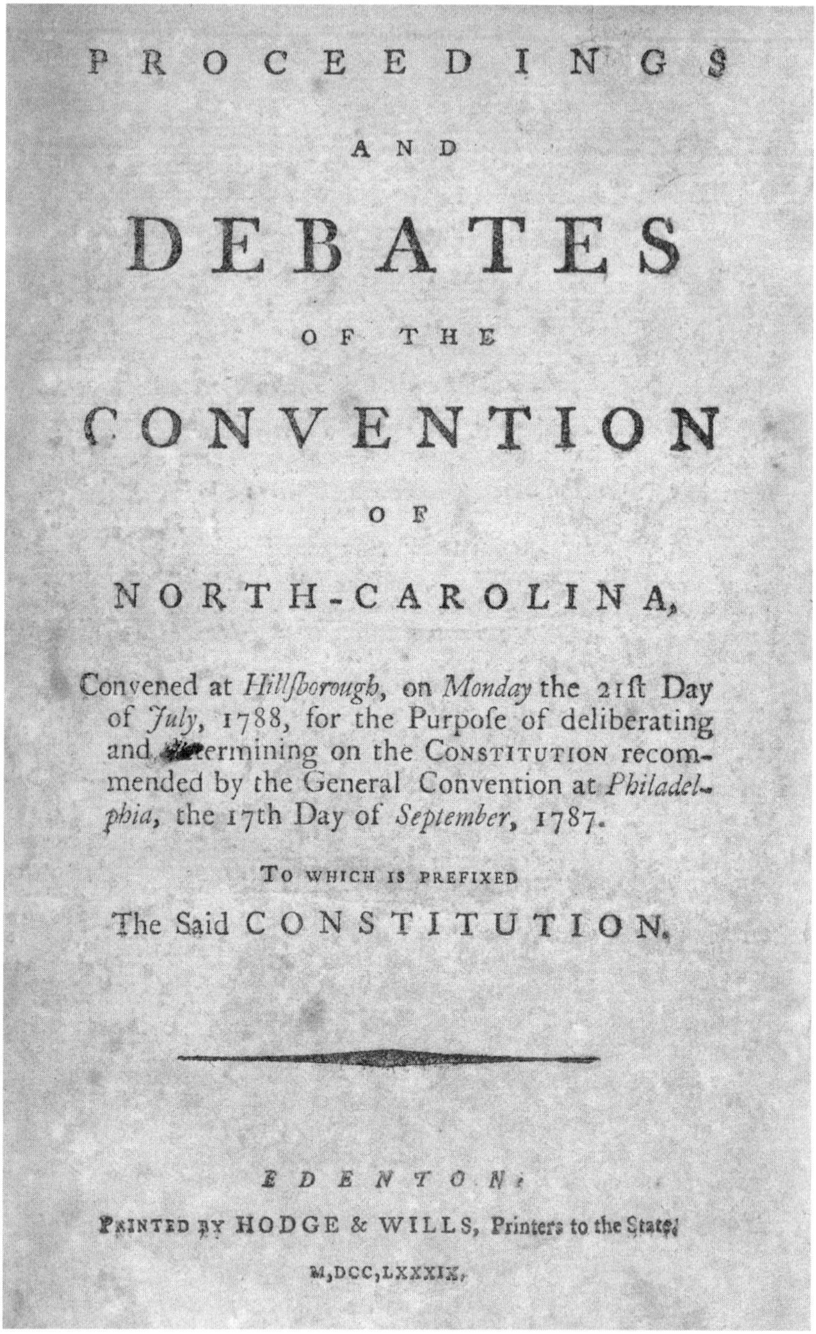

PROCEEDINGS

AND

DEBATES

OF THE

CONVENTION

OF

NORTH-CAROLINA,

Convened at *Hillsborough*, on *Monday* the 21st Day of *July*, 1788, for the Purpose of deliberating and determining on the CONSTITUTION recommended by the General Convention at *Philadelphia*, the 17th Day of *September*, 1787.

TO WHICH IS PREFIXED

The Said CONSTITUTION.

E D E N T O N:

PRINTED BY HODGE & WILLS, Printers to the State.

M,DCC,LXXXIX.

Delegates to North Carolina's 1788 constitutional convention decided that they would not ratify the Constitution without the addition of a bill of rights. This title page accompanied an account of that convention's proceedings published the following year. *(University of North Carolina at Chapel Hill Libraries)*

The Great Compromise created a Senate that would have equal representation from each state and a House of Representatives where states would have a varying number of representatives based on population. This compromise has worked well for more than 200 years.

Once the Convention had agreed on the Constitution, they had to send it to the states to be ratified. They had determined that the Constitution would go into effect when nine states had ratified it.

RATIFYING THE CONSTITUTION

As soon as the Constitution was finalized, the delegates from Delaware rushed home, and Delaware became the first state to ratify the Constitution on December 7, 1787. State after state considered and then ratified the Constitution. On June 21, 1788, New Hampshire became the ninth state to ratify, and the U.S. government took the form that still exists today. When the Constitution went into effect, there were four states left in a difficult position.

William R. Davie represented North Carolina at the Constitutional Convention and later served as governor of the state. *(Library of Congress, Prints and Photographs Division [LC-USZ62-93491])*

New York, Virginia, Rhode Island, and North Carolina had yet to vote for the Constitution. This meant they were part of the United States but had yet to recognize its new authority. Virginia and New York soon joined the other states, leaving Rhode Island and North Carolina on the outside.

In summer 1788, North Carolina held a convention to consider the national Constitution but eventually voted it down. The state constitution guaranteed the basic rights of the people of North Carolina; however, the federal Constitution did not do the same. The people of North Carolina wanted to be sure that their rights were protected by the federal Constitution. They wanted a bill of rights added before they would ratify the Constitution.

The Bill of Rights

I. Freedom of Speech, Press, Religion, and to Petition

Congress shall make no law respecting an establishment of religion, or prohibiting the free exercise thereof; or abridging the freedom of speech, or of the press; or the right of the people peaceably to assemble, and to petition the Government for a redress of grievances.

II. Right to Keep and Bear Arms

A well-regulated militia, being necessary to the security of a free State, the right of the people to keep and bear arms, shall not be infringed.

III. Conditions for Quarters of Soldiers

No soldier shall, in time of peace be quartered in any house, without the consent of the owner, nor in time of war, but in a manner to be prescribed by law.

IV. Right of Search and Seizure Regulated

The right of the people to be secure in their persons, houses, papers, and effects, against unreasonable searches and seizures, shall not be violated, and no warrants shall issue, but upon probable cause, supported by oath or affirmation, and particularly describing the place to be searched, and the persons or things to be seized.

V. Provisions Concerning Prosecution

No person shall be held to answer for a capital, or otherwise infamous crime, unless on a presentment or indictment of a Grand Jury, except in cases arising in the land or naval forces, or in the militia, when in actual service in time of war or public danger; nor shall any person be subject for the same offense to be twice put in jeopardy of life or limb; nor shall be compelled in any criminal case to be a witness against himself, nor be deprived of life, liberty, or property, without due process of law; nor shall private property be taken for public use without just compensation.

VI. Right to a Speedy Trial, Witnesses, etc.

In all criminal prosecutions, the accused shall enjoy the right to a speedy and public trial, by an impartial jury of the State and district wherein the crime shall have been committed, which district shall have been previously ascertained by law, and to be informed of the nature and cause of the accusation; to be confronted with the witnesses against him; to have compulsory process for obtaining witnesses in his favor, and to have the assistance of counsel for his defense.

VII. Right to a Trial by Jury

In suits at common law, where the value in controversy shall exceed twenty dollars, the right of trial by jury shall be preserved, and no fact tried by a jury shall be otherwise reexamined in any court of the United States, than according to the rules of the common law.

VIII. Excessive Bail, Cruel Punishment

Excessive bail shall not be required, nor excessive fines imposed, nor cruel and unusual punishments inflicted.

IX. Rule of Construction of Constitution

The enumeration in the Constitution, of certain rights, shall not be construed to deny or disparage others retained by the people.

X. Rights of the States under Constitution

The powers not delegated to the United States by the Constitution, nor prohibited by it to the States, are reserved to the States respectively, or to the people.

In fall 1789, work had begun on the federal Bill of Rights that would become the first 10 amendments of the Constitution. A second North Carolina convention to ratify the Constitution was held at Fayetteville on November 21, 1789. This time the delegates were ready to become full partners in the United States and voted 195 to 77 to become the 12th state to accept the U.S. Constitution. The state of North Carolina had to make one concession to the federal government. It gave up its claims to the lands to the west that would become Tennessee. It would take Rhode Island until May 29, 1790, to be the 13th and final state to ratify the Constitution.

The English had first begun their efforts to colonize North America under the leadership of Sir Walter Raleigh. In 1794, a new town was laid out to be a centrally located capital for the state of North Carolina. In honor of those first attempts to create a colony at Roanoke, the new capital was named Raleigh.

One of the North Carolina delegates to the Constitutional Convention, Alexander Martin also served as governor of the state and a U.S. senator. *(North Carolina Museum of History)*

North Carolina Time Line

10,000–12,000 B.C.

★ The first Native Americans are living in present-day North Carolina. By the time of contact in the 16th century, there are three Indian language groups in what will become North Carolina: Iroquoian, Siouan and Algonquian.

1524

★ Giovanni da Verrazano, a Florentine navigator working for France, explores the North Carolina coast, from Cape Fear River to Kitty Hawk. His discoveries are published in Richard Hakluyt's *Divers Voyages Touching the Discoverie of America*.

1540

★ Hernando de Soto explores the North Carolina mountains.

1561

★ Angel de Villafane, the Spanish explorer, visits as far north as Cape Hatteras.

1580s

★ Queen Elizabeth gives Sir Walter Raleigh two charters for colonies.

1584

★ **March:** Raleigh receives a patent.

★ Raleigh sends Captains Philip Amadas and Arthur Barlow to explore. They find the North Carolina coast and Roanoke Island. They bring back glowing reports of the land and people. Elizabeth knights Raleigh, and the land is called Virginia for the queen. Two Indians—Manteo and Wanchese—go to England with the expedition.

1585

★ **August:** An expedition of seven ships under Richard Grenville, along with Manteo and Wanchese as interpreters, arrives at Roanoke Island, the first colony chartered to Raleigh, under Ralph Lane. Settlers build Fort Raleigh and other buildings. The settlement is a failure, with problems from the beginning: Grenville and Lane disagree, there are problems with Indians, and a lack of food and tools. They only have only 20 days' worth of food when they land. They make it through the first winter, but the problems with the Indians are severe. A group returns to England with Drake, leaving 18 men behind.

1587

★ **June:** John White leads a second expedition, arriving near Hatteras with 110 settlers, including 17 women and nine children. They then move on to Roanoke, where they find houses built by the first expedition.

★ **August 18:** White's granddaughter, Virginia Dare, is born, the first child of English parents born in America.

★ **November:** White arrives back in England to get more supplies. A Spanish attack keeps him from returning until 1590.

1590

★ **August:** White returns to Roanoke Island but finds no sign of the settlers. The word CROATOAN is carved on one tree, CRO on a second tree.

1606

★ James I grants patents to Plymouth Company of Virginia and London Company of Virginia to colonize Virginia.

1629

★ James I's son Charles I takes part of Virginia south of Albemarle Sound and makes it a new proprietary colony, Carolana. It is granted to Sir Robert Heath, his attorney general; it extends from the Atlantic Ocean to the Pacific Ocean between 31 degrees north and 36 degrees north. Heath never acts on this grant.

around 1650

★ The first permanent English settlers arrive in North Carolina. They are "overflow" settlers from Virginia who settle in the Albemarle area of northeast North Carolina.

1663

★ Charles II, son of Charles I, grants a charter to the Lords Proprietors, eight Englishmen who helped him in his bid for the title, giving them rights to land. They rename it Carolina for Charles I.

1663–1729

★ Lords Proprietors and their descendants control North Carolina.

1665

★ A second charter is given, which clarifies the first.

1669

★ John Locke writes the Fundamental Constitutions as a model for Carolina government.
★ Albemarle County is divided into precincts; the first three are Berkeley, Carteret, and Shaftesbury.

until 1689

★ Albemarle is the only county with a proprietary government, with 12 appointed officials, a governor, and a council that the governor appoints. It has an elected assembly.

1689

★ The proprietors start appointing governors for the area of Carolina east and north of Cape Fear, the first treatment of North Carolina as separate from South Carolina.

1692–1712

★ Although Carolina is still one colony, North Carolina has its own council and assembly. The governor of Carolina is in Charleston, with a deputy governor for North Carolina.

1711

★ **September:** The Tuscarora attack, killing 140 white settlers in North Carolina.

1711–13

★ The Tuscarora War is fought in response to the terrible treatment of Indians by the people of North Carolina who have sold them as slaves, cheated them out of their land, and cheated them when trading.

1712

★ The proprietors name a governor of North Carolina, independent of the Carolina governor.
★ Pirates become a real problem, with Blackbeard and Stede Bonnet both operating out of North Carolina.
★ North and South Carolina are divided.

1728

★ Virginia and North Carolina settle their boundary dispute.

1729

★ Seven of the eight Lords Proprietors sell their land to King George II, and North Carolina becomes a royal colony.

★ Six precincts are established in Albemarle County and five in Bath County (created in 1696).

★ The settler population is roughly 35,000, with settlers from South Carolina and Virginia as well as France, Germany, Switzerland.

★ John Carteret, Lord Granville, refuses to sell his interest in North Carolina and retains economic but not the political right to a strip in the northern half of North Carolina called the Granville District, making grants to settlers.

★ The form of government remains the same during the proprietary and royal period, with a governor, council, and colonial assembly elected by voters. Colonial officials are appointed by the Lord Proprietors, then the Crown.

1739

★ Highland Scots settle the Cape Fear area.

1751

★ The *North Carolina Gazette,* North Carolina's first newspaper, is published.

1754–63

★ The French and Indian wars are fought.

1763

★ Conflicts arise between the governor and Britain. The governor has to enforce new rules designed to strengthen the colonies while keeping their colonial status.

1765

★ The Stamp Act angers the colonists.

1767

★ The Townshend Acts are passed. The Sons of Liberty are formed to pressure the North Carolina officials (but not the governor) not to enforce the Stamp Act, and groups are formed to boycott British goods to protest the Townshend Acts.

1768

★ The Regulator Movement is formed.

1771

★ **May 16:** Governor Tryon is defeated by 2,000 Regulators at Alamance Creek, effectively ending the regular government.

1773

★ **December:** The assembly starts a committee to work with other colonies. They send corn, flour, and pork to Massachusetts while it is being punished for protesting the Tea Act of 1773.

1774

★ **August:** Over the protests of Governor Josiah Martin, who would not allow North Carolina to attend the Continental Congress suggested by Massachusetts, counties and towns elect representatives for North Carolina's first Provincial Congress in New Bern. They resolve that any taxes imposed by the British Parliament are unconstitutional. They also choose delegates for the First Continental Congress, held September 5, 1774.

1775

★ **April:** The Second Provincial Congress is held in New Bern.
★ **April 19:** The Battles of Lexington and Concord, Massachusetts, are fought.
★ **May:** Governor Josiah Martin leaves his palace for Fort Johnson on Cape Fear River.

- ★ **May 31:** Citizens in Mecklenburg County meet in Charlotte, adopting a new county government, saying the king ended relations with the colonies.
- ★ **June:** Governor Martin flees to a British ship.
- ★ **August:** The Third Provincial Congress meets at Hillsboro, calling for a new colonial government with a congress.

1776

- ★ **April 12:** North Carolina authorizes delegates to the Continental Congress to vote for independence. North Carolina is the first state to do so. The fourth Continental Congress at Halifax unanimously adopts the Halifax Resolves, which call for independence.
- ★ **February:** Governor Martin tries to bring the British forces and Loyalists/Tories together in Brunswick. However, the plan fails.
- ★ **February 27:** The Battle of Moore's Creek is fought, and 1,400 of the 1,500 Tories are defeated by Patriots at Moore's Creek while en route to Brunswick.
- ★ **July 4:** The Declaration of Independence is signed by William Hooper, Joseph Hewes, and John Penn of North Carolina.
- ★ **November/early December:** The Fifth Provincial Congress meeting in Halifax adopts the first North Carolina constitution, which calls for the establishment of legislative, executive, and judicial branches of government, and a bill of rights.
- ★ **December 21:** Richard Caswell becomes the first North Carolina governor under its new constitution.

1777

- ★ **January:** Richard Caswell takes office.
- ★ **April:** The first legislature meets under the new constitution.
- ★ **April:** During the Revolution, North Carolina Patriots help to defeat the Cherokee who were on the British side, fight the Loyalists, and raise a militia of thousands. The legislature also supplies 10 regiments for the Continental army.

1780

★ **October 7:** The Battle of King's Mountain is fought along the North Carolina border of South Carolina. The North Carolina and Virginia militia defeat the British.

1781

★ **March 15:** North Carolina forces fight the British at Guilford Courthouse. The British general Lord Charles Cornwallis wins the battle, but his forces are weak, and he withdraws to Wilmington, then to Yorktown, Virginia.

1788

★ **July 21:** North Carolina's constitutional convention in Hillsboro rejects the U.S. Constitution because it does not ensure the people's freedom. They adopt resolutions with amendments and a bill of rights. The U.S. government starts without North Carolina.

1789

★ **November 21:** The second convention at Fayetteville, North Carolina, adopts the U.S. Constitution, becoming the 12th state to accept it.

North Carolina Historical Sites

BATH

Historic Bath Bath was the first town established in what became North Carolina. It remains a small town, with numerous historic buildings. Tours of two of the buildings, the Palmer-Marsh and Bonner House, are available.

> *Address:* P.O. Box 148, Bath, NC 27808
> *Phone:* 252-923-3971
> *Web Site:* www.ah.dcr.state.nc.us/sections/hs/bath/bath.htm

BURLINGTON

Alamance Battleground On May 16, 1771, royal governor William Tryon and his army of 1,000 defeated the 2,000 Regulators who were rebelling against the royal government at the Battle of Alamance. A visitor center houses an audiovisual presentation on the battle.

> *Address:* 5803 N.C. 62S, Burlington, NC 27215
> *Phone:* 336-227-4785
> *Web Site:* www.ah.dcr.state.nc.us/sections/hs/alamance/
>   alamanc.htm

EDENTON

Historic Edenton   Historic Edenton has been called "the South's prettiest town" and was an important political center in the 18th century.

> *Address:* P.O. Box 474, Edenton, NC 27932
> *Phone:* 252-482-2637
> *Web Site:* www.ah.dcr.state.nc.us/sections/hs/iredell/ iredell.htm

HALIFAX

Historic Halifax   Historic Halifax features a guided walking tour that allows visitors to enter several historic buildings, including a 1760 merchant's house as well as a jail and a tavern.

> *Address:* P.O. Box 406, Halifax, NC 27839
> *Phone:* 252-583-7191
> *Web Site:* www.ah.dcr.state.nc.us/sections/hs/halifax/ halifax.htm

MOUNT GILEAD

Town Creek Indian Mound   Town Creek Indian Mound gives visitors a glimpse into pre-Columbian life in North Carolina.

> *Address:* 509 Town Creek Mound Road, Mt. Gilead, NC 27306
> *Phone:* 910-439-6802
> *Web Site:* www.ah.dcr.state.nc.us/sections/hs/town/ town.htm

SANFORD

House in the Horseshoe   Originally the home of Colonel Philip Alston, commander of Whig troops, it is now open to the public.

> *Address:* 324 Alston House Road, Sanford, NC 27330
> *Phone:* 910-947-2051

STATESVILLE

Fort Dobbs   Although Fort Dobbs, the site of several battles during the French and Indian War, was dismantled in 1764, there are displays of artifacts, as well as archaeological sites and trails.

> *Address:* 438 Fort Dobbs Road, Statesville, NC 28677
> *Phone:* 704-873-5866
> *Web Site:* www.ah.dcr.state.nc.us/sections/hs/dobbs/
>   dobbs.htm

WINNABOW

Brunswick Town/Fort Anderson   Founded in 1726, Brunswick was named after George I, a king of England who was born in Brunswick, Germany. Today a visitor center has displays on the town's history.

> *Address:* 8884 St. Philips Road SE, Winnabow, NC 28479
> *Phone:* 910-371-6613
> *Web Site:* www.ah.dcr.state.nc.us/sections/hs/brunswic/
>   brunswic.htm

Further Reading

Books

Alter, Judy. *The North Carolina Colony*. Chanhassen, Minn.: The Child's World, 2004.

Britton, Tamara L. *The North Carolina Colony*. Edina, Minn.: ABDO Pub., 2001.

Fradin, Dennis. *The North Carolina Colony*. Chicago: Children's Press, 1991.

Lacy, Dan Mabry. *The Colony of North Carolina*. New York: Watts, 1975.

Lefler, Hugh T., and William S. Powell. *Colonial North Carolina: A History*. New York: Scribner's, 1973.

Uschan, Michael V. *North Carolina*. San Diego: Lucent, 2002.

Whitehurst, Susan. *The Colony of North Carolina*. New York: PowerKids Press, 2000.

Worth, Richard. *North Carolina*. Danbury, Conn.: Children's Press, 2004.

Zepke, Terrance. *Pirates of the Carolinas*. Sarasota, Fla.: Pineapple Press, 2000.

Web Sites

North Carolina Museum of History. "North Carolina Museum of History." Available online. URL: www.ncmuseumsofhistory.org. Updated on January 30, 2004.

North Carolina Office of State Archaeology. "North Carolina Archaeology." Available online. URL: www.arch.dcr.state. nc.us. Updated on March 24, 2003.

State Library of North Carolina. "Historical Highlights of North Carolina." Available online. URL: http://statelibrary.dcr.state. nc.us/nc/history/history.htm. Updated on May 8, 2003.

State Library of North Carolina. "North Carolina Historic Sites." Available online. URL: http://statelibrary.dcr.state.nc.us/nc/ ncsites/list.htm. Updated in May 1996.

Index

Page numbers in *italic* indicate photographs. Page numbers in **boldface** indicate box features. Page numbers followed by m indicate maps. Page numbers followed by c indicate time line entries. Page numbers followed by t indicate tables or graphs.